W9-ABC-989

SD
387
.W6
B73
1983

Brett, Richard M.,
1903–

The Country journal
woodlot primer

DATE			

BUSINESS/SCIENCE/TECHNOLOGY

© THE BAKER & TAYLOR CO.

THE COUNTRY JOURNAL
WOODLOT PRIMER

THE COUNTRY JOURNAL WOODLOT PRIMER

The Right Way to Manage Your Woodland

by Richard M. Brett

Country Journal
Publishing Company, Inc.
Brattleboro, Vermont 1983

Copyright © 1983 by Richard M. Brett

All rights reserved under International and Pan–American Copyright Conventions. Published in the United States by Country Journal Publishing Company, Inc., 205 Main Street, Brattleboro, Vermont 05301.

Distributed to the trade by W. W. Norton & Co., Inc., 500 Fifth Avenue, New York, New York 10110.

Illustration Credits

Pages 57, 62 (bottom), 72, 73, 76, 77, and 80: Aldren Watson
Pages 34, 49, 61, 98, 102, and 104: Ray Maher
Pages 62 (top), 64, 66, and 68: Margot Apple
Pages 37, 39, and 41: Robin Brickman
Pages 99, 100, and 106: Elayne Sears
Page 60: Edward John Brown
Page 87: Gordon Morrison

The map on pages 10–11 is from *Fruits and Berries for the Home and Garden,* by Lewis Hill. © 1977 by Lewis Hill. Reproduced by permission of Alfred A. Knopf, Inc.

All photographs are by Clare Brett Smith except the photograph on page 111, which is by the author.

LIBRARY OF CONGRESS CATALOGING IN PUBLICATION DATA

Brett, Richard M., 1903–
    The Country Journal Woodlot Primer.

    Includes index.
    1. Wood-lots—Management. 2. Wood-lots—United States—
Management. I. Blair & Ketchum's Country Journal. II. Title.
SD387.W6B73   1983   634.9'28   83-7481
ISBN 0-918678-04-8

Manufactured in the United States of America

First Edition

10 9 8 7 6 5 4 3 2 1

For Elizabeth

CONTENTS

THE COUNTRY JOURNAL
WOODLOT PRIMER

1 | 🌲🌲

Introduction

I WRITE THIS book because small forests, or woodlots, are among our most valuable national assets—and among our most neglected. Books on forestry are generally pitched to the scientific management of large commercial forests; woodlots of a few acres that will never yield great wealth to their owners are passed over by most writers on the subject. This is a pity, because our woodlots are in a deplorable condition for the most part, and there is great need for informed management of them by their owners.

There are tens of thousands of private woodlots in the United States and Canada, ranging in size from a couple of acres to a couple of hundred. Many of the owners of these woodlots are aware that they have charge of an important resource—a potential producer of forest products, of cash, and of a lifetime of study and recreation. But, usually, their woodlots are uncared-for, or worse, they are cut over indiscriminately or sold for real estate development; not because the owners were unaware of their value, but because they didn't know how to take advantage of it. Owners have not the vaguest notion where to start, what to do, or how to do the work that may be involved in assessing and realizing the value of their forest property.

Those woodlot owners who have tried to learn a little about

I

forest management have found that they had to plunge right into heavily technical forestry texts and into the driest kind of how-to manuals. They have also found that most forestry has a purely economic lean, and that the management of forests for other than cash gain—for improved wildlife habitat, for recreation, for simple beauty—has been neglected. Woodlot owners who haven't wanted to study the fine details of forestry, and whose motives in improving their woods have included other elements than profit, have had little in the way of advice from writers on forestry.

This book is intended to guide and advise the small woodlot owner in setting about a program of woodlot management for improved yield of forest products and for other, less tangible, improvements as well. It is not a minute how-to book, and it is not a text. Readers who want detailed information on tools, on tree identification, on log scaling, on forest pathology, can find it elsewhere. This book is an introduction, a primer. It will give you a clue, a pointed finger. It will start you out in woodlot management, and it will help you to evolve your own solutions.

I approach the subject of woodlot management in an unorthodox way in this book; unorthodox in that my approach is personal rather than strictly scientific, and in that it is not exclusively commercial. In my work in forestry over thirty years, and in writing this book, I have been guided by the principle that a woodlot is much more than a site on which to grow trees that will be cut as soon as possible for man's use. Rather, a woodlot is a complex biological whole—an entity—that must be used with intelligence, but above all with care and respect. It follows that it is immoral as well as unwise for us—as individuals or as a nation —to exploit our forest resources to the full in a single generation. We must practice the ethic of *stewardship* with respect to our forests, and we must see ourselves as their keepers, not their owners. We hold our forests not freely, but in trust for future generations. In this book I hope to help the woodlot owner put the stewardship principle into practice on the small—but to him and to us all, vital—scale of his own woods.

Anyone who sets himself up as an author on a complex and important subject ought to say how he came that way and what makes anyone think he has anything to say worth hearing.

I suppose forest work is built into my genes. My father, George P. Brett, came from a long line of Kentish farmers, and was transplanted to this country at an early age. As a grown man, around 1908, he moved from Darien, Connecticut, to nearby Fairfield because he thought Darien was too crowded. In Fairfield we lived on a proper farm. There were oxen and draft horses for power, and the wind to pump water; pigs, chickens, ducks, geese, and turkeys abounded. There were gardens and orchards, and we raised barley, rye, oats, corn, and buckwheat.

My father's, and my own, main enthusiasm on the farm, though, was the *pinetum*, or collection of evergreens. Father collected seed from all over the world and tried to grow many non-native evergreens in Fairfield. When I was home I was often the truck driver who collected special trees, and I often helped with planting, watering, and pruning jobs.

The Brett Pinetum long ago succumbed to progress; today executive homes with pools and tennis courts fill our arable land and supplant some of my father's rare trees. Nevertheless, Elizabeth, my wife, and I did save several acres of fir. This area is now owned and managed for genetic research by the Yale School of Forestry.

Somehow my early experiences have made me into an avowed generalist. Although at college I majored in literature, my first jobs were in banks. I moved on to work in book publishing, followed by a stint as a lieutenant colonel in the Air Force during World War II. After the war I was the first manager of the business end of the New York Public Library.

At fifty I renounced the business world and entered the Yale School of Forestry and Conservation for two years, aiming to become a forest ecologist. I graduated in 1955. At that time Yale had a marvelous program in forestry, as it has today. If the university accepted your project, you could sample any course that Yale had to offer. I took most of the forestry courses and dabbled in such matters as the uses of mass media for public education and the wonderful oddity, limnology.

After graduation, to put all this new learning to the test, Elizabeth and I established the Hawk's Hill Demonstration Woodlot on some two hundred acres in central Vermont. As in other woodlots in the state, the land was neglected, and the woodlands, from a commercial point of view, were producing only a fraction of the value that they ought to have produced. We set out to prove that ordinary care would improve this yield appreciably and that intensive management of forest plantations would lead to major increases in yield of forest products. We also thought that, while achieving these commercial goals for the woods, we could protect the land, improve water quality, nurture wildlife, grow Christmas trees, and enjoy and promote the best kinds of recreation.

It worked. The trouble was that by the time Hawk's Hill had begun to prove itself we were getting too old for the day-to-day work of forestry. We had been doing all the work of planting, pruning, cutting, road-building, and so on. We turned the project over to the New England Forestry Foundation of Boston, Massachusetts. NEFF's resident forester continues the work. There's a lesson here, too. It takes a long time to create a good woodlot. An individual will hardly be around long enough to complete the job. Still, do not rush. If you decide to give nature a hand in the woods, do it, but do it gently. This book will help to show you the way.

What Woodlots Are

HAVING STATED MY purposes, it is time to get down to some specifics. How big a piece of property do I have in mind when I talk about a woodlot? What makes a woodlot? How do woodlots come to be?

SIZE

The answer to the question, How big should a woodlot be? is kind of like Mr. Lincoln's answer when he was asked how long a man's legs should be. "Long enough to reach the ground," Lincoln said. So it is with woodlots. Size is relatively unimportant within certain limits: the woodlot owner's purpose and the care he gives to the land are the important things about a woodlot, not its acreage.

Nevertheless, I ought to assure the reader that we are not talking about commercial forests of several thousand acres, whether natural or planted. Neither are we talking about suburban back

5

yards. Let's say that for our purposes a woodlot is a forested tract between ten and two hundred acres in area.

Why the *lower* limit? Can't you have a half-acre woodlot, or a six-acre woodlot? Well, not really. A forest under about ten acres is too small to have any reasonable economic purpose. Even if the lot were full of good-sized trees, no logger could ever be induced to harvest such a small area; it just wouldn't pay him to do so. *Exception:* If the trees in this tiny forest were of an unusually valuable species—walnut, say—or if they were unusually large and perfectly formed and were therefore salable as "peelers" (logs from which furniture veneer is made) then the forest might have a commercial value. For the most part, however, the smallest wooded properties are too small to yield a significant return from the sale of logs or other forest products; which is why I insist that a woodlot must be ten acres or larger.

The upper limit on the size of a woodlot is more movable than the lower. I said two hundred acres. I might have said three hundred, or more. The point is that above a certain size a woodlot ceases to be manageable by one person. He'll have to hire people to work in the woods, or to plan for various sections of the forest. He'll have to invest in a lot of specialized machinery. The forest will be too big for one person to compass and care for on his own. That doesn't sound like a woodlot any more, at least it doesn't to me.

Now that I have said what a woodlot's size requirements are, and insisted that size doesn't really matter so much, it is time to move on to some requirements of woodlot-hood that do matter. Now it begins to get interesting.

WATER

It is impossible to have a natural woodlot without water. Nearly all our productive woodlands receive at least fifteen inches of precipitation per year. The precipitation can be mist, rain, snow, sleet, even dew. It helps if the precipitation is distributed more or less evenly throughout the year; although some trees do adapt to rainy seasons alternating with dry ones.

Second- or third-growth hardwoods. A hillside woodlot in Barnard, Vermont.

North America is a well-watered, and therefore a well-wooded, continent. Precipitation will support tree growth over the United States and Canada except in the desert regions of the Western states and the barren lands of the Northwest Territories. Whether particular areas support *woodlots*, however, depends on factors other than precipitation, not all of them natural factors.

SOIL

After water the next most necessary condition for growing trees is soil. Vegetables can be raised in chemical-rich water solutions. I daresay you might even grow a tree or two that way—but a hydroponic woodlot would be a hard place to love.

Soils are sweet or sour. Sweet, or alkaline soils were usually the bottoms of prehistoric lakes or seas, whose animal inhabitants, dying over millions of years, contributed calcium from their shells and other parts to the mineral material on the sea bottom. Sour, or acid soils are remnants of prehistoric swamps or bogs; their acidity comes from vegetation decaying over the eons. Volcanoes, glaciers, and weathering by wind and water have worked on the "original" soil materials to produce local soil conditions.

In North America the most important families of forest trees are pretty widely distributed over different soil regions. Nevertheless, not every kind of tree will grow in every kind of soil; soil composition and chemistry can *promote* the growth of certain kinds of trees, although they may not *exclude* trees of other kinds. For example, sandy soils, with adequate water, favor the great pine forests of New Hampshire and northern Michigan. Broadleaf, or hardwood trees often grow in these soils, too, however, with the pines. Again, the limestone soil of the Ohio Valley favors the growth of what were once the greatest hardwood forests in the world, although pines and spruces grew in that region, too, in spots where special conditions permitted them to take hold.

TEMPERATURE

In an area where precipitation and soil permit the growth of trees, temperature affects what *kinds* of trees will grow more than any other factor. Foresters have made weather zone maps for the continental United States and Canada. No rule is ever unexceptionable. Some local condition—a confluence of rivers, a large lake, a seashore, a steep-sided valley—will vary the temperatures widely. The altitude and exposure of a site also help determine its average temperature: high ground is in general colder than low; ground with a southern exposure is relatively warmer than ground oriented northerly.

Nevertheless, despite local deviations, the broad temperature zones are valid. They extend across the United States and Canada following the fact that our weather moves from west to east. Zone 1 on the temperature maps does not interest us, for trees do not grow in this zone. Zones 2–10 do interest us, and they are defined by mean minimum winter temperatures, thus: Zone 2, -50 to $-40°F$ mean minimum winter temperature; Zone 3, -40 to $-30°F$; Zone 4, -30 to $-20°F$; Zone 5, -20 to $-10°F$; Zone 6, -10 to $0°F$; Zone 7, 0 to $10°F$; Zone 8, 10 to $20°F$; Zone 9, 20 to $30°F$; Zone 10, 30 to $40°F$.

Different tree species have adapted to life in different temperature zones. This adaptation is never perfect or perfectly predictable, however. Nature is constantly fooling man, and certain anomalies exist—witness red spruce in the Carolinas, a tree of the far north that fled south to get away from the glaciers and found a home, and sweet gum in Vermont, where it does not belong, according to the rules of cold.

Because of such anomalies, and because local conditions modify average temperature, the cold zone system is not going to pinpoint what you will find in your woodlot, no matter what zone it may happen to be in. The factors which will decide what grows where will include zone, altitude, proximity to large bodies of water, degree of slope and which way the slope faces, soil type, and water. Nevertheless, as I said earlier, temperature is the main

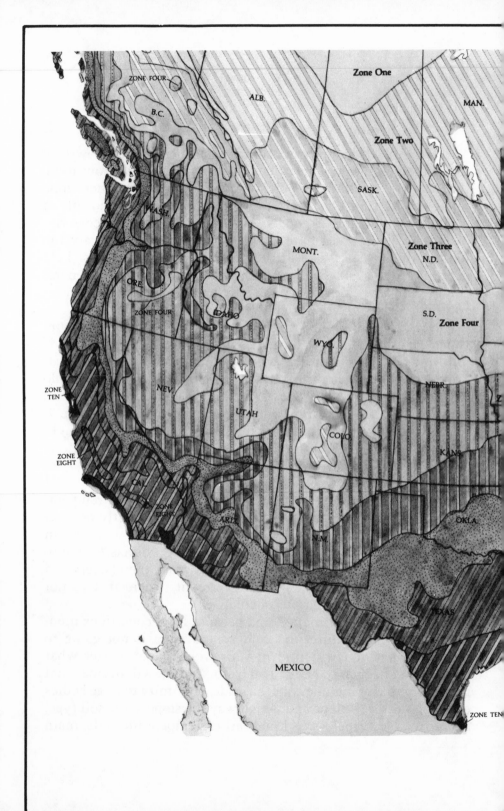

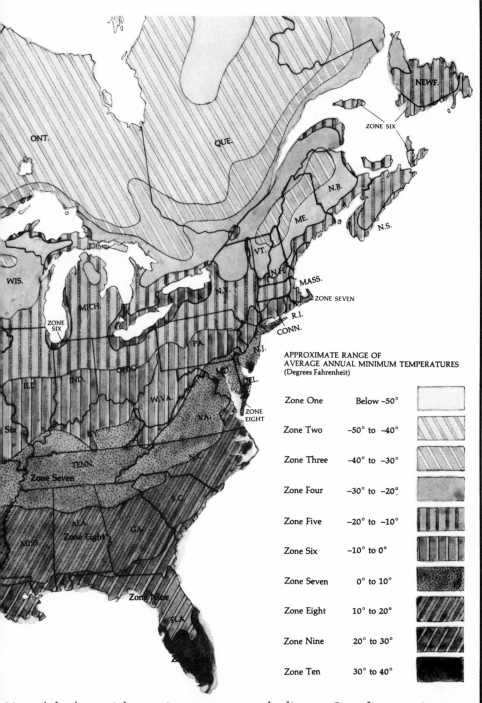

APPROXIMATE RANGE OF
AVERAGE ANNUAL MINIMUM TEMPERATURES
(Degrees Fahrenheit)

Zone One	Below –50°
Zone Two	–50° to –40°
Zone Three	–40° to –30°
Zone Four	–30° to –20°
Zone Five	–20° to –10°
Zone Six	–10° to 0°
Zone Seven	0° to 10°
Zone Eight	10° to 20°
Zone Nine	20° to 30°
Zone Ten	30° to 40°

Map of the forty-eight contiguous states and adjacent Canadian provinces showing temperature zones, or areas of similar annual mean minimum temperatures.

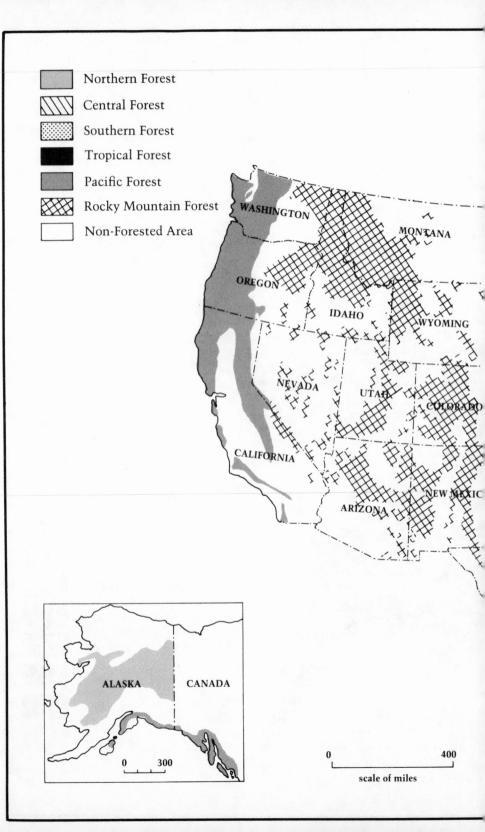

Northern Forest
Central Forest
Southern Forest
Tropical Forest
Pacific Forest
Rocky Mountain Forest
Non-Forested Area

WASHINGTON
MONTANA
OREGON
IDAHO
WYOMING
NEVADA
UTAH
COLORADO
CALIFORNIA
ARIZONA
NEW MEXICO

ALASKA   CANADA

0   300

0   400
scale of miles

Forest Zones of the United States

orest zones. In contrast to the temperature zones, which run roughly east-west across the continent, forest zones run roughly north-south, in part reflecting changing altitude.

factor behind the distribution of kinds of trees over the land—or what grows where.

Tree species are divided into groups according to the temperature zones where they flourish. The groups include northern hardwoods, with certain accompanying evergreens; transitional hardwoods, which may be a bewildering mix of species that stray from one group to another; and southern hardwoods and their own evergreen friends. Which of these tree groups grows in an area determines the *forest zone* that area is in. Like the temperature zone map of North America the forest zone map is not perfectly regular—far from it; but irregularities, again, are largely owing to temperatures. For example, the northern hardwood forest extends deep into the southern hardwood zone along the heights of the Appalachian Mountains where lower temperatures prevail in the southerly regions.

LAND OWNERSHIP

Along with water, soil, and temperature, a fourth factor may determine whether woodlots will be found in a given area, and this factor has to do less with biology than with history. The existence of woodlots depends on the existence of small (ten to two hundred acres, remember?) holdings of wooded real estate; and these are not found commonly in all parts of the land.

They are common in the Northeast. There, long ago, real estate speculation was practiced on a broad scale. England wanted to export some of its people and wanted to establish them in the new country, so grants of land were given to wealthy peers who proceeded to set up towns without much knowledge of or regard for terrain. These speculators sold or gave land in relatively small parcels to people who would come overseas and settle on the land. Another reason for the division of the Northeast into small holdings was the gift of land to Revolutionary soldiers. The country was bust and had no other way to pay off those who had fought, so the land was broken up in small tracts and deeded to veterans. This pattern of land ownership resulted in many small farms. When the farms were later abandoned, the land—which by 1860 had been mostly cleared of trees—reverted to forest, but the land ownership remained, generally, small. Maine, which is a very large state for the East, does have some large forest areas owned by lumber and paper companies; but the norm in the other northeastern states is small woodlots.

Similar patterns developed in the mountainous parts of the South and in the northern tier of states. In the Deep South, however, the institution of slavery resulted in large land holdings; and elsewhere in the South and Southwest, the French and Spanish influences were strong and did not favor small holdings. When some Western territories were being prepared for statehood, there was an attempt to promote small ownership by limiting land and homestead grants to some 160 acres. Ways were soon found, however, to combine these small plots into bigger units—too big for woodlots to be common. Also, much forest land in the West remained in the hands of the federal government and was never divided into small holdings.

There are woodlots in every state and province. If you own a woodlot, however, chances are it's in the northeastern quadrant of the country—including New England, New York and the other Mid-Atlantic states, and the Midwest.

DIVERSITY

The last characteristic of woodlots I'm going to talk about is the one that is to me paramount, and in stressing it I give away a fundamental principle of mine. It is this: Biologic diversity equals biologic strength. Woodlots, to be healthy, should be diverse. They should contain different kinds of trees, of different ages, growing in different conditions. Diversity helps to ward off disease and pests. If there are many kinds of plants in a woodlot, there will be, automatically, many different kinds of insects, birds, and beasts. There will also be different diseases; but there will not be a concentration of any one tree to provide a banquet for pests or diseases bent on the destruction of the whole. There

are just too many different kinds to permit an epidemic, normally.

Where there is not diversity—the spruce-fir area of Maine, for example—or where man has created a monoculture, there is a tasty banquet laid for enemies of the trees in the monoculture. With large quantities of favorite foods in front of them, the insect populations respond with considerable enthusiasm. Their population curves rise rapidly and tend to stay at peak as long as there is a supply of the host tree. Eventually, under normal conditions, these insect populations will attract their own destruction through the growth of their own predators or parasites. Meantime, however, their predations in monoculture forests encourage man to try short cuts by spray programs. Spraying delays the regular cycle of natural pest control because the sprays are not selective, and they kill friend and foe without discrimination.

Diversity means resilience. Diverse forests can recover from fire and uncontrolled or clear-cut logging more quickly and with less help from us than can forests in monoculture, natural or manmade. Following a burn or cutting, specialized plant and tree species ("pioneers") take hold on the bare ground, grow up quickly, and prepare conditions for the eventual return of other —usually larger and more valuable—trees. Seeds of these pioneers must come from somewhere. In a big single-species forest —especially one managed for commerce—where diversity is discouraged, pioneer seeds may have to come a long way. In a diverse woodlot, they are apt to be growing right there in the first place.

Biologic diversity equals biologic strength. *Corollary:* Right management of woodlots should aim at encouraging diversity.

At present I am the owner and manager of a subcompact, six-acre woodlot in my Vermont village. (I know: I said a woodlot had to be ten acres or bigger. Read on, anyway.) There's no money to be made from such a postage-stamp woods. But I have the woodlot under intensive management, nonetheless. My aim is to make biologic diversity a reality. When I bought the property in the late 1950s, it was being invaded by poplar, good for pulpwood sale in quantity, but no good for my purposes. As it happened, I

Red pine stand (planted 1947) in the Hawk's Hill Demonstration Woodlot, Barnard, Vermont.

was at the time growing different species of the northern hardwood complex in a nursery. I cut the poplar and introduced the better hardwoods, and, if the site seemed to be right, conifers, too. My present venture, then, is not economic but a sort of scientific effort to place as many native trees on these six acres as possible. In a later section I refer to this effort in detail as an arboretum or special collection of native trees.

At the time I had charge of the two-hundred-acre Hawk's Hill Demonstration Woodlot the idea was the same: to promote biologic diversity. I aimed to create a good habitat for wildlife, make a place for recreation of several sorts, and improve the quality of the trees so that I could sell high-producing forest products such as peelers and piling (long, straight trees whose trunks are driven into the ground to retain land fill or make foundations for structures). In the process I hoped to find a market for every tree that I cut. Some would be cut for fuel. Some, in plantations of evergreens, might very early on in the thinning be sold for Christmas greens and trees. Further thinnings might go for pole buildings, pine cabin material, or pulp.

At Hawk's Hill, Elizabeth and I—and our successors, the New England Forestry Foundation—wanted to show that one man with appropriate tools could use a woodlot to increase his forest capital, obtain firewood and lumber for his own use, make periodic sales to help pay his taxes, insurance, and other cash needs of this sort, and still run a general farm or even a dairy.

In order to prove that this was possible for anybody who wanted to try, we hired no outside help. Our cultural work and construction work were done in times when the average Vermont farmer has time to work in the woods. We felt that there were about two weeks' time in the year when the regular farming operations were not breathing too hotly down the farmer's neck and that he could well afford about a week in late fall and a week sometime in the winter, depending on weather conditions, to work in his woods. He could, as we did, set blocks of the woods for special pleading—thinning, firewood cutting of culls, pruning in softwoods, occasionally harvesting trees for the sawmill, and so on. In doing this work, some extra time could properly be spent in making access roads and skid trails.

The stimulus was a statistic. At that time, a typical acre of

Vermont woodlot was producing about $1.50 per acre per year. We set out to triple that yield, at least. We thought that $25 per acre per year might be possible on superior sites.

You know, it worked.

The Hawk's Hill Demonstration Woodlot was an experiment in growing better trees faster than Nature would do it on its own. As I have remarked, trees do not grow like radishes. Nature often takes over a hundred years to produce a harvestable tree. By thinning, I aim at a forty-year cycle in the plantations and perpetual yield in the hardwoods.

The plantations—white pine, red pine, and white spruce— were watched carefully. When the growth slowed, thinnings were made by the value judgment method. Any tree that crowded a better tree, any tree that was damaged in any way, or any tree that was not making good growth, was treated as a cull and removed; but some use was found for those removed in the thinning. Trees cut from the plantations provided fence posts and highway guard posts. Sometimes the thinnings were used for pole buildings or log cabin stock. As an aside, I made two open-face shelters for the Skyline Trail at Amity Pond, near Hawk's Hill, from trees that Elizabeth and I had planted as seedlings. Either red or white pine were used for this purpose. Thinnings from the hardwoods produced stove wood or wood used to boil maple sap. Sometimes a cull would also contain a saw log or two. The object was to find some use for every discard and for this use to contribute to the overall economic gain of the woodlot. The method was to apply imagination to woodlot management, taking diverse products from woods in which diverse trees had been planted or allowed to grow wild. In managing woodlots I aim to help nature; nature thrives on diversity, and therefore my work with nature must be diverse as well.

III | 🌲🌲

What Woodlots Do

THE MOST IMPORTANT thing that woodlots do for us is not to grow the lumber that builds our homes; it is not to grow the fuel that heats our homes; it is not—even!—to grow the trees that make the pulp that makes the paper that made this book. The most important thing woodlots do for us is to provide pure water, and provide it in benign amounts. Water and woodlots are inextricably interrelated. Without water, as I have shown, woodlots couldn't be; without woodlots—or forests—flood and drought would make much of the earth uninhabitable.

WOODS AND WATER

Water is nature's most powerful tool. With gravity and water, all mountains are destined to become plains. Every reader will have seen in his own experience the awesome power of flood. But probably few will have noticed how small are the beginnings of flood. A single drop of water falls from a height. Photographs show that the single drop makes a tiny depression in unprotected ground. As the water splashes out of this depression, it carries minute amounts of soil with it. On any slope (and, by the nature of things, there is no such thing as absolutely level land) this single drop with its soil burden rolls downhill. It is joined by billions of similar drops all carrying bits of dirt. The force of this moving mass picks up more and more load and soon the drops start to coalesce into streams, brooks, and rivers—flood waters, bent and determined to level the land, by their own sheer force, and by the abrasive action of their soil load. Sometime, if you are in the mountains near a rapidly moving stream, you can hear the boulders in the bed load sliding and banging their way downhill. The final volume and force are immense.

Whether by happenstance or divine plan, forests slow the gathering of floodwaters to a turtle's pace. Forests, including small woodlots, protect the soil against the impact of falling water, the small beginning of flood. Much water that falls in a forest never reaches the ground. Rain and snow lodge among leaves and branches and are quite quickly evaporated back into the air. The water that does fall to the ground in a woodlot is held; it doesn't run off—or at least it doesn't run off as quickly as it would from unforested ground.

Run-off from bare soil is almost total. Grass slows the rush of water. Forest soil, however, holds water and controls flood better than anybody's Corps of Engineers. How is this miracle accomplished? By the nature of forest soils. I am not implying that forest soil contains some special ingredient that holds it together on a steep slope. Many characteristics of forest soil contribute to its water-holding properties.

The forest floor is a complicated place. Its terrain is uneven. Some trees are shallow-rooted and blow over quite easily. Some trees are exposed to windthrow and fall over. Some trees are downed by a combination of events—an ice storm, wind, heavy rain, and so on. When a tree does fall, its roots rise out of the ground taking a big plug of earth with them and leaving a hole where the roots formerly stood. This depression traps water and organic materials. Much water, so trapped, seeps into the ground. Roots do not live forever. When they die, they decay, leaving veins into which water may enter. Burrowing rodents, for their own purposes like seeking grubs or burying nuts, make small water passages into the soil. The forest floor is rough and full of holes, crannies, and passages. These slow run-off and provide for water entry. Some of this water is used by the trees in the growing process, but some of it is saved for ground water reservoir.

Forest soil is like a great sponge—efficient at holding water. The *duff*—fallen branches, twigs, leaves, dead undergrowth—that covers the forest floor makes a loose, porous cover that allows water to percolate easily into the soil below. This water is released as seeps and brooks; but the forest releases it *gradually*, and not as a rushing flood.

Forest soils also help to purify groundwater by acting as a water filter. The water that passes slowly through the earth of a woodlot, to emerge in a spring or creek, will have been cleansed—of silt, and even of many pollutants. Run-off water from inadequately forested land is murky, full of soil in suspension. Sound familiar? It should. It's the condition of many of our rivers. It has been said that the wide Missouri is too thick to drink and too thin to plow. Forest streams are clear.

When we preserve forests—when we preserve woodlots—we are preserving good water and protecting our land against flood at the same time. It is a vast tragedy that forests today are being cut down heedlessly all over the world, for the consequences will be grave.

In the Northeast we are apt to congratulate ourselves on our increasing use of wood for home heating over the last ten years or so. We should reflect, however, that wood-burning has its dark side. Sixty per cent of mankind today uses wood for cooking and heating. Wood cut for these purposes by poor rural people in Africa, Asia, and India is not replaced. As lowland forests are cut away for fuel, less accessible forests on higher, steeper slopes must be cut. The result is increased flooding, increased erosion, decreased potable water. Nobody should believe that the same results won't follow here if wholesale cutting of forests, for whatever purpose, becomes the rule.

Formerly, it was the rule. Our pioneers thought that the forests were without limit, and they thought trees were their enemy: The land must be cleared. They did not know what role the forests played in providing water, in forming wildlife habitat, and in

Pruning in a pine plantation, this one dating from about 1953.

softening the effects of wind and the elements in general. They cut the woods recklessly wherever they went, and the result was flooding, erosion, and extinction of local forest wildlife.

Today we're supposed to know enough not to do this, but we do it anyway. We're greedy. Many of our wood-using industries, and even trained foresters, who ought to know better, occasionally think of a tree as immediate money to be had right now if the market is good. These institutions and individuals sometimes have no regard for the next generation and totally ignore the ethic that man is merely a custodian and, therefore, should not exploit every resource, here and now, for short-term economic gain.

SOIL

After its role in flood control and water production, the next most important thing a forest does is to produce soil. Water and organic soil are the basis of our survival on earth. Where does the soil come from? Put simply, it is ground-up rocks and organic matter. The organic stuff is the magic part: it's that that grows our food, and most everything else. Most of the organic component of soil comes from decaying vegetation. From the soil's point of view, a forest exists to supply dead leaves, trees, and undergrowth to be turned into soil.

All leaves on all trees die, usually every year. The leaf fall of the deciduous trees is especially dramatic, but the evergreens also lose their needles. The larch loses its needles annually. Other evergreens shed continuously, a little at a time so it is not noticeable. Bits of bark, twigs, branches, and mature trees fall. It is estimated that two tons of this material fall on every acre of a fully stocked forest every year.

The minute a leaf falls it is attacked by a host of agencies of its destruction. Rots, moulds, all manner of insects, as well as rodents and billions of microbes start to work on the material and to turn it into soil. This is the way of all life and, viewed in this way, it is a form of immortality. It beats Phoenix rising from its own ashes all hollow for efficiency.

I do not want you to get the idea that soil formation takes place overnight. It is not like your compost pile, or even like mine. The kind-hearted sexton of the neighboring cemetery gives me all the cemetery leaves every year. I put them in piles, one pile for each year. I add garden refuse and vegetable stuff from the kitchen waste, and at the end of three years I put this through a mulcher and arrive at almost the same sort of material that forms naturally in woodlands. But nature's methods—frost, rain, snow melt, plus animal remains and bacterial action—take much more time. Some soil scientists say that a working forest in good condition builds about an inch of soil every hundred years. (In the tropical rain forests, however, things move faster: There, soil is being built and used constantly because growth takes place throughout the year and there is no seasonal pause as there is in our forests, which rest quietly under the snow for several months.)

Everything that a forest does—every part of a forest's life—is connected to everything else and to every other part. A forest's soil- and water-work are an example. The forest builds soil, and the forest protects the soil by restraining run-off and preventing erosion. The water that the forest soil retains contributes to the growth of the forest, which furnishes new material for soil-building. It is a harmonious and efficient system.

FOREST PRODUCTS

Some wag once said that if wood did not exist naturally, we would have had to invent it. This is a sly way of saying that wood is a versatile material. Making small woodlots yield useful and salable products is the subject of most of this book; and I won't dwell on that subject here. Instead I will make the summary point that woodlots are, ideally and by nature, diverse in the products they can be made to yield; this diversity reflects the principle discussed earlier, that in woodlots biologic diversity equals biologic strength.

Woodlots can furnish lumber, pulp, fuel, furniture wood, veneer wood, pilings, Christmas trees and greens, and packing materials like excelsior. These are products made from wood directly. Woodlots also produce maple syrup and sugar, and honey; and, a bit farther afield, anything that can be made from fossil fuels can be made from wood by fractional distillation.

I trust nobody smiled when a moment ago I put Christmas trees and greens on the list of forest products right there with lumber, furniture wood, and pulp. Maybe the raising of Christmas trees is not usually a woodlot project, but I made it one at the Hawk's Hill Demonstration Woodlot. I planted Norway and white spruce for pulp as the first crop and for dimension lumber in the final stages. I planted them on six-foot centers, and if the survival was good, they were too thick. The thinnings went for Christmas trees and greens.

The best woodlot management takes the variety of a woodlot's potential products into account. Good woodlot management *does not* seek to squeeze the biggest amount of money from the woodlot by overexploiting one product at the expense of others. You don't cut all maples for lumber if you want to sugar, even if maple is bringing high prices at the mill this summer. Instead, you try to learn what products your woods might yield, and then you try to balance the harvesting of different products. In this way you work in phase with the diverse functions of your woodlot, and you ensure that it will be producing a like variety of good things after you are gone. That is good woodlot management, and it is good custodianship: careful, foresighted, intelligent.

RECREATION

A woodlot is a complex biologic entity that uses the power of the sun to produce vegetation, build soil, and control and purify water. In so doing a woodlot—inadvertently, so to speak—provides a habitat for animal and plant life—including man. I have tried to show how the diversity of habitat provided by a woodlot can be important in protecting it from pests and disease. But wildlife habitat is also an important advantage of woodlots for people who would enjoy them.

I suppose hunting has more devotees than any other forest-using kind of recreation; but woodlots also welcome hikers,

Small Christmas tree plantation at the author's home in Woodstock, Vermont.

skiers, campers, birders, botanizers, photographers, artists, and a million others.

Woodlots do not welcome one class of recreationists, however, at least mine doesn't. I refer to those who rely on motorized equipment: snowmobiles, motorcycles, off-road vehicles. These things are a bane, in the woods especially. Snowmobiles permit man to invade the woods at the very time that wildlife survival is being put to the severest test. Even if the snowmobile user refrains from harassing deer and other animals, the machine's noise, smell, and very presence cause stress for the animals and force them to use energy, burning up fat reserves and making later winter survival even more precarious. Bikes and off-road vehicles also disturb and frighten wildlife, but the main reason to ban their use in the woods is that these vehicles strip the water-holding organic cover from forest subsoil, and thereby promote erosion. I think that it is necessary to exclude these machines from any woodlot.

While I am engaged in annoying the macho mind, I may as well go ahead and put my oar in on the side of beauty as an important resource in any woodlot.

Woodlots can be orderly and relatively tidy. Woodlots can aim to look like the primeval forest. I saw a virgin forest once, in Nova Scotia many years ago. The trees, through competition, had spaced themselves so that each survivor had its share of sunlight and forest floor. Natural pruning had left these trees with straight and limbless boles for dozens of feet. There were some ground covers and some wildflowers, but the principal feeling was of space, and there was a wonderful, soft footing caused by an accumulation of organic soil covered almost completely by a carpet of springy moss.

When a woodlot owner uses his intelligence and energy wisely, he can make beauty in the woodlot as well as an ideal place to grow trees. The beauties of a woodlot can be viewed and enjoyed at any time of the year, from the winter of Robert Frost's famous poem about his neighbor's woods filling up with snow to the early spring days when hardwood buds and flowers spread a colorful haze overhead and the ground is spotted with wildflowers busy going through their blooming in haste before deep shade ends their day in the sun.

Summer woods are different. They form a dark and sometimes mysterious cavern, cooler than the adjacent meadow. An ancient hymn points up this difference by saying that the woodlands are fairer. I agree. Not even a poet or an artist can do justice to woodlands in the fall. I will not try. There are compensations in woodlots, however, even for nonartists. If one is practical minded and somewhat practiced in the art, one can in autumn, for example, do a fine job of tree identification, sitting on the terrace, drink in hand, perhaps. The poplar is new-minted gold. The swamp maple is scarlet and indicates wet spots on the hillside. The sugar maple shows in yellows, oranges, or reds depending on the nature of the site. An ash often looks like royal purple, but you have to watch sharp. The ash tends to drop its leaves all at once. I was at my kitchen window one fine fall day enjoying the colors. By some unknown force, a large ash started to lose its leaves. In ten minutes it was bare, and I had witnessed a fall of royal purple.

When the trees are bare, snow or no snow, one can see the architecture of individual trees and the stratagems by which they provide a platform for the display of the leaves which, in summer, will power the manufacture of wood and store energy for next season.

In a woodlot there is beauty for every season and, to my mind, the lift of the spirit that a woodlot can give is necessary for the sanity of man, especially for those who live their crowded lives in an economic world where ignorance, greed, and the misuse of technology hold sway.

INTERCONNECTEDNESS

A few pages back I suggested that the functions of a woodlot— including water retention, soil-building, habitat formation— were all related to and dependent on one another. It follows that what affects one element in a woodlot affects all the others eventually. For this reason, right woodlot management must be slow and deliberate, and must avoid drastic measures of every kind.

Unfortunately, man tends to ignore this admonition when he wants to turn woodlots into money. Some trained foresters are afflicted with dollar signs in their eyes and perpetrate much harm because of a limited and short-sighted approach to their work.

If a woodlot is carelessly clear cut, for example, many relationships in the woodlot are destroyed. Water hits unprotected soil and causes erosion and siltation from uncontrolled run-off. This water is no longer available to enter the ground and replenish ground water supplies. The habitat of many creatures is no more, and the effect of this change is not predictable. Even the quality of the soil is changed. It is no longer moist and mellow. The hot sun penetrates quite deeply and even changes the chemical composition of the soil.

While clear cutting may be economically profitable in the short term, especially in even-age monocultures, it does present dangerous change, and for that reason it is almost always to be avoided in a woodlot. I think that the only time clear cutting is justified in a woodlot, as differentiated from a large commercial forest, is if the owner wishes to eliminate some species which is not valuable for his purposes. For example, I used to clear cut small plots of gray birch and red maple. Neither met my plans, and neither is of value except for firewood. These small quarter-acre clear cuts were very useful in enhancing the habitat for varying hare, grouse, and deer. The openings provided available sprouts much enjoyed by all three creatures.

In the woodlot the watchword is Easy Does It. Don't try to overcome the diversity of the woods; rather, be guided by it to diversity of woodlot activities and products. Aim always at soil stability and water production and protection. Bear in mind constantly that working in a woodlot should be a long-range project. Woodlots move slowly. A mature tree may arrive at saw log or veneer status at the end of sixty to a hundred years, and as we've seen, it takes a hundred years to build an inch of forest soil. Go slowly, for then you are more apt to go carefully.

IV | 🌳🌳

Learning About a Woodlot

YOU HAVE BEEN reading for a little while, puzzling out an admittedly unorthodox approach to woodlot management. Now it's time to *do* something. Get out in your woodlot, see what's there, and begin to plan what you're going to do with it.

Take along your survey map, which shows the boundaries of your property. You don't have a survey map? Get one. Don't make your own (unless you are a surveyor). The survey should be done by a registered surveyor to meet legal requirements as well as practical ones. Cutting, road making, and other woodlot work on land that turns out not to be your own is to be avoided.

CULLING

Map in hand, walk to a corner of your property or to a spot where there is ready access to a road. By pacing, measure off a rough square about two hundred feet on a side. This approximation of an acre will do for our present purposes. Mark off the sides and corners of the square with brightly colored surveyor's tape,

33

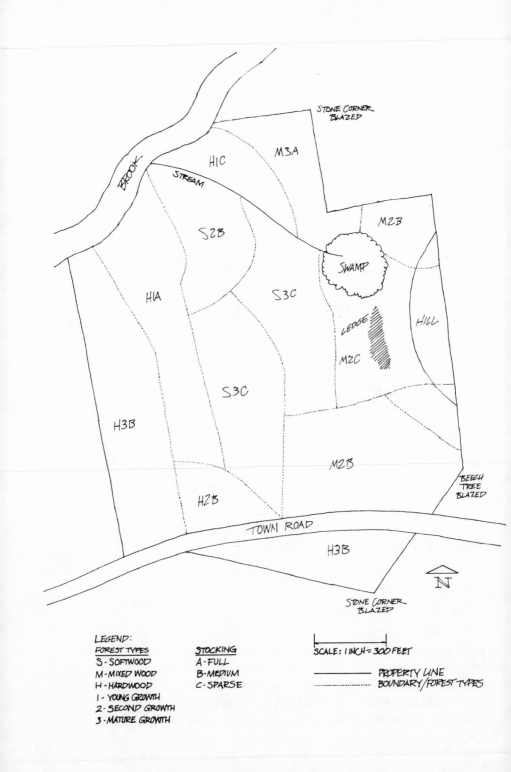

STONE CORNER BLAZED

M3A

HIC

STREAM

BROOK

M2B

S2B

SWAMP

HIA

S3C

LEDGE

HILL

M2C

S3C

H3B

M2B

BEECH TREE BLAZED

H2B

TOWN ROAD

H3B

N

STONE CORNER BLAZED

LEGEND:

FOREST TYPES
S - SOFTWOOD
M - MIXED WOOD
H - HARDWOOD
1 - YOUNG GROWTH
2 - SECOND GROWTH
3 - MATURE GROWTH

STOCKING
A - FULL
B - MEDIUM
C - SPARSE

SCALE: 1 INCH = 300 FEET

———— PROPERTY LINE
.... BOUNDARY/FOREST TYPES

or strips of waste cloth, or by spray-painting trees (please don't blaze trees with an axe; it doesn't do them any good, and you can't see the blazes at any distance). Mark the location of the square on your map.

In your square acre of woods the job you have now to do can be done in any season, but late fall is perhaps the best time for it. A light November snow on the ground (what deer hunters call a tracking snow) will help to show you where you have been; and hardwood leaves will not block your view.

Your tool is a long, strong stocking filled with dry lime or flour. Walk to a back corner of the square and stop ten feet from the back line. Walk parallel to the back line, looking around. Go slowly, and look for trees that are not pulling their weight. One may be big enough for a saw log, but it leans, taking up too much space. Another tree may have a broken top damaged by an ice storm or by lightning. Porcupines may have gnawed patches of bark from a third tree. "Conks" (fungi) may appear on a fourth. Machinery carelessly handled may have damaged the bark or the root structure on other trees, or mixing cows and forests may have resulted in root damage. An ancient fire may have swept through the woods and left a number of trees with burn scars, sometimes known as cat faces. Such trees represent the present harvest for fuel, pulp, or lumber. To get the idea of what the woods might be like if these trees were removed, swat each tree with your stocking *on the side facing you.* This will permit you to review, at a glance, what you have marked for removal. After finishing the first row, step back ten feet or so and repeat the process, and so continue until you have reached the point where you entered your square acre. Look back now over the marked area. The swat marks will stand out, and you can judge whether you have marked enough, or, maybe, too much for the first time around.

You don't want to open the stand too much at first by culling too many trees. In hardwoods too many are cut if there are large

Simple sketch map of a woodlot. This map was adapted from a timber-survey map drawn for a woodlot owner by the New England Forestry Foundation. Note the Legend keyed to the map to show forest types and stocking in the woodlot.

The author swat marks a tree to be culled in his woodlot in Pomfret, Vermont.

openings between tree crowns. Large openings will admit too much sunlight, which will lead remaining trees to put out sprouts all along their stems ("epicormic branching," so called) causing small knots. In softwoods excessive culling producing large openings in the forest canopy can lead to sun scald and wind throw. Sun scald of trees is very much like sunburn of people: tender vegetation is actually burned by intense sun. Wind throw is a more serious threat, especially in softwoods. Softwoods are, generally, shallow-rooted trees. In the woods they lean on one another for support, their branches intertwining. Opening up a stand excessively removes this support from many trees and allows wind to get into the stand. Trees, unsupported, may be blown down.

Cull trees. Defective trees with swollen trunks, poorly healed wounds, and many ragged branch stubs are normally useless as sawlogs and may be culled for firewood.

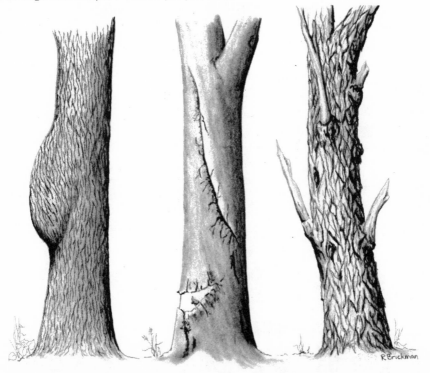

It's also possible to cull too few trees. When you've finished your first tree-marking pass through your first square acre of woodlot, look up. Imagine the look of the canopy if the trees you marked were gone. Too few have been marked to cut if crowns look meshed with each other and growth appears to be slowing. You can't tell easily whether tree growth is slowing in a woodlot, of course. Foresters have a special tool that drills into a tree trunk and removes a core of wood. The tree's annual growth rings, visible in the core, indicate growth rate: thinner, closer-together rings—slower growth. You don't need such a tool. It is easier to look up and make a value judgment about degree of crown density. If the crowns are very close together and overlapping, cull more trees. The tree tops should just touch fingers.

It is graver to err on the side of too much culling than on the side of too little. Therefore, as you look back over your white swat marks you should plan to take it easy and not try to accomplish too much the first time.

I suppose a sharp reader will say that I have not mentioned, in the previous exercise, anything about spacing of trees in the

Conks or fungi on a hardwood trunk—a sign of decay within—indicate a candidate for culling.

The drawing at top left shows a woodlot before culling. Succeeding drawings show the same woods thinned suitably for wildlife habitat only, for saw timber only, and for wildlife and saw timber, both.

woodlot. I have not done so on purpose because I do not believe in arbitrary rules in this subject, or, for that matter, in anything else. I believe in reasoned judgment applied to the subject at hand.

There are all manner of theories and arbitrary spacing rules in forestry. I do not use them, because they are complicated; because they ignore local site conditions and terrain; because various species have various ways of growing and of occupying the land. I say, Look, and make your own subjective judgment. For all I know about your woodlot, and what you prefer, you may put esthetics high in your methods and choices. In one section of my woodlot, the sugar maples tend to grow in clumps. These are not sprouts from an old stump. In these groups the trees are quite close, within three to five feet, but each individual is proceeding heavenward at a good clip and putting on girth in the bargain. It would be silly to try to apply an artificial mathematical spacing rule here. If the trees in your woodlot are thriving, help them, not by spacing but by the elimination of inferior competition.

WHAT TO KEEP

It would be sensible to repeat the cull-marking exercise described in the last section in several places in your woodlot so that you get a feel of what is to be cut and where. You are culling to remove trees that are defective or otherwise undesirable, and to promote the growth of valuable or potentially valuable trees. What's valuable depends on what you want. All trees may be valuable; but man has his favorites. Some trees fit man's purposes better than others. One woodlot aim is usually to promote rapid growth of trees that provide firewood, pulp, lumber, veneer, and pilings. You need to examine the acre of woodlot you have marked and determine which healthy, well-formed trees are present that have value for these uses. This examination will guide your work in the woodlot.

If and when you start the actual cutting of culls, the product will probably be mostly fuel wood. Be not proud. My woodpile contains every kind of tree I have cut. I do not like waste, either,

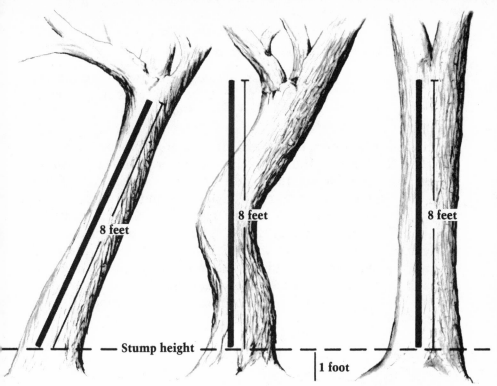

Sizing up sawlogs. Learn to look at trees in the woodlot with a view to determining how much saw timber they'll produce. In this drawing the trees on the left and right will each yield an eight-foot sawlog, with the tree at right being an ideal sawlog candidate and the one at left being only passable. The crooked tree in the middle is useless for saw timber.

and while gray birch is nasty to handle, it will burn in a stove. I cut it and use it, along with elm, pin cherry, poplar, and all the other culls that I make in weeding my woodlot. The only expenditure is that of labor, and the way I choose to spend my time is my own affair. I do not have to earn any basic wage per hour so long as the product of my labors is beneficial to me now in fuel wood, and so long as it is beneficial to me in the future in increase of my forest capital.

Pulpwood, in the past, came largely from spruce, fir, and poplar. Now some of the hardwoods are also utilized for pulp. It is hard to generalize, but the pines, usually, are soft and easy to work and so have been used for walls, partitions, and finish lumber. Spruce and hemlock, being stronger than the pines, were used for supports of many kinds, sometimes called dimensional lumber.

Various oaks, beech and sugar maple were used where their strength and density were valuable. Oak and sugar maple often went into flooring. Several of the oaks were used for framing buildings.

Trees useful for lumber must be big enough to produce sawlogs. How big this is is in the eye of the beholder to a degree. Some loggers cut veritable saplings and call them sawlogs, and some mills buy them if the market is hot. The standard sawlog is 16 feet, 4 inches long and no less than 12 inches in diameter at the small end; although sawlogs can be 8, 10, and 12 feet long, too. It really comes down to what your local mill will buy at the time you want to cut the tree, and market conditions, species, need to cut, and intended use of the log all affect this.

The two best paying forest products are veneer stock

A peeler, in this case a long, straight ash suitable for being made into veneer. Such trees are among the most dependably valuable in most woodlots.

("peelers") and piling. I mentioned these in Chapter II. Almost any large, straight, sound, and relatively knotless wood can be sliced or peeled into very thin layers to be used for furniture and wall covering—sometimes, but not always, sandwiched under pressure with less expensive woods. In the woodlot, veneer candidates are fast growing, undamaged, straight, relatively limbless trees of superior species. These are your best crop trees: to the extent that you are managing your woodlot for harvest you are managing it to protect and encourage the growth of these trees and their offspring. Piling stock are tall, straight, and limbless softwoods, quite often red pine, which can be driven into harbor mud or swamp land to retain fill to make new land or to serve as building foundations. Such wood, covered by mud or wetland, will last a long time. Prices for piling are not always as high as prices for veneer stock, but when contractors need pilings they need them, and they will pay well for them. A forester (you're about to meet him) will advise you on current local markets for pilings and other forest products.

I won't try to tell you in detail which woods call the highest prices. There are too many variables. Prices change from day to day, species to species, place to place, mill to mill—all influenced by styles, inflation, market conditions in general, the prosperity of the building trades, weather, and a host of other matters. (Case in point: ladies wore stiletto heels, maple prices high; ladies switched to wedgies, maple flopped, pine rose sky high.) An up-to-the-minute price sheet is what you need if you are going to try to peddle logs. And even then, do not cut until you have a firm price. Many a poor man has cut on a say-so, and when his logs reached the mill has found the owner of the mill doesn't need any now but will take them off the cutter's truck "at a discount," meaning for peanuts. Get a firm price from the mill, with a deposit if possible, at the time of cutting.

In going through your woodlot for valuable species, don't let the price of peelers blind you to other kinds of value. I said a little while ago that all trees may have value. Delete the "may." There are no weed trees, really. In New England, where I live, gray birch and poplars, locally known as popple, are the main contenders for the title. I used to think that the hop hornbeam was the real weed. Then I learned that poplar and hop hornbeam are favorite

food sources for partridge, so I changed my mind. Poplar can be sold for pulp. It can be made into fine kindling. The Swedes make matchsticks out of it. As for hornbeam, it used to be called leverwood, and it is virtually impossible to break and is a dandy fuelwood. So, if you have a poor site with full sun it might be sensible to favor these weeds. Staghorn sumac is not really a tree, nor is it a shrub. It is a nuisance, but its function is to prepare the land for real forest trees. It, too, has its uses. It makes good kindling. An old plant can be cut into thin boards for small doodads like boxes.

USING A FORESTER

Now it is my duty and pleasure to introduce you to the indispensable man, or woman—one, by the way, whose help can make the foregoing woodlot examination and evaluation far easier and more informative than it is likely to be if you embark on it alone. I refer to the professional forester. The forester is a different breed of cat from the folk who like to pass themselves off as being practical wood cutters and even skillful loggers. He has, or he should have, scientific training and a degree in forestry.

The forester will come from either the private or the public sector. If he comes from the public sector he is probably a county forester, which means that his clients might be any persons who own forest land in his county. County foresters' services are free, but they are like the salesman's winter overcoat: you don't buy it, but you do pay for it. You pay for the county forester with your taxes. These foresters are well trained, dedicated public servants; they are overworked. Their time must be available to any landowner who seeks it. They can be hard to get hold of when you need them, and the time they can devote to each landowner is limited.

The private, consulting forester is just as dedicated and just as well trained in his profession as the county forester. Furthermore, he is your man. To earn his pay, he must do what you have

The author, left, is indicating a straight, well-formed young red pine of the kind suitable for piling stock.

requested, when you want the work done. As a steady diet, I would recommend the private forester.

One does need to take care in selecting and working with a forester. Common honesty is not as common as it is supposed to be. In every profession and in every walk of life, there are people with itchy palms. There are also some professional foresters with a narrow view of their profession and some who are blinded by dollar signs in their eyes. Beware. Learn about foresters in your area from other woodlot owners, and pick one whose reputation is high. Your forester must have personal integrity. He must be your man, and he must not be tied in any way to a mill owner, a machinery operator, or a group of wood cutters.

Any forester can do any or all of the following services. He can make a land survey and a map; a timber inventory by species with estimates of the proper allowable cut (which should not exceed the annual growth rate except in a salvage operation); he can cull or thin a woodlot; he can prune; he can prepare a cutting contract with a logger; obtain bids from loggers who will do the cutting; supervise the cutting and preparation work, which might include laying out roads and landings; he should police slash disposal and verify the mill count. No matter what he is to do, the arrangement from start to finish should be in writing.

It is usually a good idea to enlist a forester's participation in your woodlot projects early in the game; you might even invite him along on your first tree-swatting tour of your measured acre. The forester can give you better help if he's involved from the outset than he can when he's called in to retrieve a woodlot program that is already well along on the wrong course.

KNOWING YOUR WOODLOT

With a forester and alone, get out in your woodlot and get to know it in all seasons before you start on any programs of wood harvesting that is at all extensive. Look at your woodlot with a critical eye in the different seasons. In winter, when the hardwoods are free of leaves, it is easier to see defects and "sweeps"

—leans from the vertical or a bow effect in the bole—either of which can reduce a tree's value as timber. Frost cracks and lightning strikes also damage trees for lumber. In winter these are easy to spot. Tops broken by an ice storm reveal themselves, as do the big bald spots in tree bark that porcupines chew off. Fire-caused cat faces are hard to spot in winter, however, because the snow tends to hide them.

Look for den trees—big, old, dead or partially dead individuals that harbor birds and animals. A den tree is a condominium catering to borers and other wood-loving insects, grubs, and decay agents of every kind. These attract squirrels, chipmunks, mice, and woodpeckers, which in turn attract owls, weasels, and other predators. Porcupines frequent the premises, so do raccoons. I have even known a skunk family to take over a ground apartment. All of these life forms depend to one degree or another on the den tree, and they all add to the diversity of life in a forest. If you care for wildlife in your woods you will not only spare these unprepossessing old stubs, you'll give them as wide a berth as you can in your woodlot work.

In the spring and summer get out in the woods and look for brooks and wet places. You won't find many of these places in winter, but you need to know where they are, for you'll have to avoid or otherwise overcome them with your access roads later on. Look also for ledges, walls, large deadfalls, and other obstacles to maneuvering in the woods, that may be hidden in winter.

Please don't think I want you to have your mind sternly on business every minute you're in the woods. Far from it: you should be seeing more than the outlines of a future timber harvest. If you hanker for wild honey, summer brings out the bees, and they give the location of their store away by their busy goings and comings. Summer and fall bring on the mushroom crop. Each year and each soil type has its own colorful array of fungi. Beware, some are poisonous; but also rejoice, many are delectable.

In the fall it is pleasant to shuffle slowly through the fallen leaves. When they are dry, the muted noise is nostalgic. All these benefits are yours to enjoy as you work and plan in your woodlot. Your job has more and better perquisites than that of the senior vice president of the most overstuffed corporation I can think of.

CHOICES

When you have been around your woodlot a bit and have learned in a rough way what trees are there and what their quality is, you're about ready to set to work; but if you're smart you'll wait. Before you gas up the chainsaw and wade in, reflect that when you know what's in the woods you only know half the equation. The other half is *you*. What do you want of your woodlot? What will you want in five years? In twenty? What will your children want? You have some choices to make in defining your purposes in the management of your land. Doing the job in your head or on paper is a lot easier than rushing into the field, chainsaw in hand, only to find you're making mistakes.

There are limits to what kind of management a woodlot can have. Some of them are imposed by the size and character of the woods in question: you won't be harvesting saw logs from two acres of alders—at least not for a while. Other limits are your own. You are constrained by limits on your time, money, ability, energy, and degree of interest. Nevertheless, for practically every reader, whatever his time, financial, and personal limitations, there is a range of choices he can make for the management of his woods. The range is from minimum intervention in the woodlot to maximum intervention.

DOING NOTHING

Every military man knows that doing nothing—taking no action, sitting on your hands—is itself a choice, with consequences of its own. In forestry, however, doing nothing is okay, whereas in war it's usually a mistake. Deciding not to make an effort to change what is happening in your woodlot is a perfectly reasonable choice. Be not satisfied, however, with just ignoring the woods. Rather, try to learn from them: describe the woodlot as it is and record changes from year to year in a journal or forest diary.

To keep your forest diary, you'll need an accurate census of the trees in your woodlot: what trees of what sizes are there, in what numbers? How precise this inventory is depends on you. Some foresters count, map, and describe every plant in a given area. Some mark off several plots—as you did on your survey map in the tree-culling exercise in the last chapter—choosing the plots to be typical of certain plant associations, and then inventory them, extrapolating from the census plots to the woodlot as a whole. You can get as nit-picking as you want about this: what's important is that you have a clear and fairly detailed idea of what trees your woodlot supports. Having achieved this, you watch and wait, employing *curiosity* as your woods tool in place of louder, cruder implements.

The fact that you are doing nothing in your woods is very far from meaning that nothing is happening in them. Any woodlot,

The drawing shows stages in forest succession, with bare ground growing up to weeds at the left and succeeding to "pioneer" tree species (pines, here), young hardwoods, and mature hardwoods at right.

as I have suggested, is constantly changing. You're in a position to see and record the changes in your woods. The most conspicuous of them are changes associated with forest succession, or the reclaiming of open land by forest trees. The order in which trees of different species invade a clearing, eventually returning it to forest, is determined by a host of climatic and soil factors. In my bailiwick old fields grow up first to a dense crop of poplar saplings, because poplar bears light seeds which travel easily on the wind and because poplars demand direct light to grow. However, poplar is short-lived and usually does not replace itself. It acts as a forerunner or nurse for the establishment of more permanent forest trees, usually hardwoods in the northeast. If nothing is done, when the poplar dies off, it will be replaced by more permanent species. Which these are will depend on the usual variables: prevailing wind, neighboring seed sources, altitude, soil type, and exposure.

The observant woodlot owner is in a perfect spot to learn about succession patterns. Ten years ago an acre of twenty-year-old red pine plantation of mine was blown down. The soil was thin, and the slope where the pines grew was considerable. Came high winds and heavy rains, and my pines were knocked flat. What to do? I decided to do nothing and see what happened. We salvaged the down wood for fence posts, but intervened in no other way. Immediately nature started a reclamation process of its own. Milkweed, dock, and goldenrod took over, followed by wild berries. By five or six years after the blow-down, cherry, maple and birch seedlings were established. Interestingly, no pines came to replace the pines that had blown down, demonstrating that this is hardwood land.

Without lifting a hand to modify your woods, you can witness the life and death of forests and fields. No one really knows how forest successions work out in detail everywhere, year after year; there are too many variables, and since trees live longer than men, complete observations need to stretch over generations. This is rare. Your forest diary—well kept up—may have scientific value some day.

Brush and young hardwood pioneers beginning to reclaim open land for forest.

WOODLOT MANAGEMENT FOR PRODUCTION AND RECREATION

At the opposite end of the woodlot-management spectrum from doing nothing but observe is *intensive woodlot forestry,* management in which a variety of products are taken from the woodlot in a harvest that is pretty well continuous. The theme of this book is the benefits that accrue to small woodlot owners who institute a course of intensive woodlot forestry, and so I will not restate these benefits in detail here. Suffice it to say that an intensive woodlot forestry program can give you perpetual yield and increased forest capital, but only at the cost of lots of time and hand labor from you—time which can never pay you even minimum wage. As I have suggested earlier, woodlot owners who want to get rich quick are reading the wrong book. But if you enjoy woods work, have time for it, are content with small forest income to help pay taxes or the like, and have a yen to improve your land, intensive woodlot forestry will reward you hand-somely.

Between doing nothing and the full practice of intensive wood-lot forestry, there are many alternatives. You can harvest fire-wood only; you can harvest a single crop such as lumber or pilings; you can hire a woods-butcher who will high-grade your woods, taking the good trees, ignoring the poor ones, and leaving you with a wasteland; you can go for maple sugar. You may be able to sell pulpwood. In the old days, pulpwood—wood used in paper making—was softwood, but today most any wood is used by pulp mills. The advantage of selling pulpwood is that any trees, however misshapen, can serve for pulp as long as they are more than about seven inches in diameter. However, selling pulpwood is usually feasible only for woodlot owners who are ninety miles or less from a paper mill and who can furnish a predictable annual cut—again, large forests and large-scale for-estry operations are favored by pulpwood buyers.

Managing woodland in the spirit of intensive woodlot forestry is usually compatible with the recreational use of woods. Trail making and habitat improvement for wildlife can be part of your forestry plan, and they can help your woods yield extra enjoyment for you and others. I'm not going to go into these for-fun extensions of woodlot management here; they have a chapter of their own later on.

Any ostensible summary of the choices you can make for using your woodlot suggests that only uses on the list at hand are okay. I would avoid suggesting that in the foregoing. The choices I've described—from not intervening in the woods at all, to taking various forestry measures, to improving wildlife habitat and recreational potential—are ones I've tried myself here and there. They can be combined; they can be modified; they can be ignored and entirely new plans made. The idea is to give you a notion of the riches in experience as well as in lucre that a woodlot can be made—quite easily—to yield.

V | 🌲🌲

Tools and Tasks

ABOUT THE ONLY creature that can accomplish much work in the woods without tools is the beaver. I once had a crew of beavers working for me at the Hawk's Hill Demonstration Woodlot. I imported several to the property and invited them to take over a small brook where the upper reaches were grown up in a stand of poplars that were in my way. The beavers removed them efficiently and with nearly perfect selectivity. On the basis of this experience I can recommend beavers as woods workers. Nevertheless, the recommendation must be qualified. As employees, beavers are not the steadiest workers (they slack off in the winter, for one thing). All in all, therefore, I guess I'd better say that if you're going to be working in your woodlot you'd best not rely on rodent helpers; get yourself some hardware.

In describing woods tools I'm not usually going to specify brands or particular sizes or styles to buy. Instead, I'm going to suggest classes of tools and let you do the selecting depending on your own preferences and on what is available in your area. Call on tool and hardware dealers. Ask them what local woodsmen and loggers use. Be guided by their experience, and then buy according to what weights, sizes, and styles of tool fit your own tastes.

CLIPPERS AND LOPPERS

To start the tool list, I always stick a pair of stout hand clippers in my hind pocket. Some small branch is forever poking into a trail, lying in the path of your axe swing, or blocking your path. I find a pair of sensible hand clippers equipped with a safety catch the easiest way to remedy such problems.

In addition to one-handed, pocket-sized clippers, I often use two-handed, long-handled clippers, or loppers, for swamping out around a tree to be cut or clearing a retreat path from beside it. These loppers come in several models and weights. I like the kind with sliding levers which serve to multiply the force of your own arms in closing their jaws. These loppers will cut through anything you can jam into their jaws. I think their higher cost is worthwhile. My pair is still going strong after thirty years of rough usage. They do not owe me anything.

I know that experts look down on me for using clippers and loppers. They use an axe. They bend a sapling and neatly and cleanly sever it with no misses, fusses, or feathers. That is not my class. I am forever banging into things, hitting the only stone in Vermont. This sort of thing is not axe-beneficial.

AXES

I use an axe for splitting firewood, for limbing felled trees, and for dealing with branches or small trees that obstruct my way; but not for felling trees, bucking up large firewood logs, or any of the other big jobs for which the axe was once the only tool. I must say that I am not man enough to buck up wood with an axe, and I cannot imagine how people in the 1600s and 1700s cleared our hardwood forests with axes alone. The art is not lost,

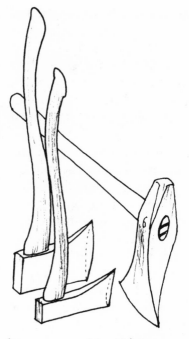

Axes. The larger of the two axes shown standing up is a heavy, conventional poll axe, and the smaller is a light Hudson's Bay axe best used for cutting small limbs and brush. The third tool shown is a splitting axe or maul.

however: a friend of mine makes his living competing in chopping trials. He is over forty, and I find his skill with the axe remarkable, though it must once have been commonplace.

The earliest mass-produced axes came into use in the early 1800s. There were hundreds of varieties, weights, and sizes. Today most stores stock no more than two or three varieties of axe. It is said that a narrow, thin axe blade cuts best in hardwood and a wider blade is best for softwood. Maybe so. I haven't noticed much difference. I own three axes: a big, heavy one with a $5\frac{1}{2}$-pound head and a 30-inch handle for splitting firewood; a light, short, Hudson's Bay model axe that I keep in my car trunk and use on troublesome fallen branches and to get up campfire wood; and a Connecticut model axe just a little lighter and shorter than the splitting axe, which I use for limbing felled trees.

No hatchets, please. The hatchet is a carpenter's tool; it is out of place in the woods. Anything you might use a hatchet for in the woods you can do with an axe or hand saw more efficiently and more safely. With its short, one-handed swing, the hatchet is hard to guide, and a miss can easily damage your delicate anatomy.

For splitting very fat and knotty firewood I have a splitting maul—a kind of axe-sledgehammer hybrid with a maul-like head formed into a dull, narrow axe blade at one end and a flat striking face at the other. My maul has an 8-pound head and measures 36 inches in length. The extra weight of this tool allows you to cleave all but the toughest firewood billets, and the hammer face of the head lets you drive steel splitting wedges for the most stubborn pieces.

Another permutation of the axe that is not for me is the double-bitted kind, logical as this tool may be. One side of the head is kept sharp for fast, clean cutting; the other is kept duller for rough cutting where you might hit a spile, a bit of wire, or an unseen stone. I suppose I shy away from the double-bitted axe because I am really not a first-class axeman. It is so easy to part your hair with the side of the blade which is not cutting wood at that moment. I think that the double-bitted axe is for the expert and for the macho young. When I was in forestry school, my classmates all had double-bitted axes which they kept razor sharp. But they were children, and I was a retread of fifty—I knew better. No double-bitted axe for me, then or now.

You may not want to start out buying three axes. If I could have only one, I'd have the Connecticut-style limbing axe, which has a rounded blade that cuts clean and seems to resist nicks; this might be the place to start for you. When you buy any axe, make sure the head is firmly seated on the handle. Avoid axes with brightly painted handles: the paint often conceals crooked, weak wood grain or splits. And avoid axes with "unbreakable" handles of fiberglass. They'll break, all right, and when they do you'll have to buy a whole new axe, for you can't simply replace the broken "unbreakable" handle as you can with a wooden-handled axe.

Any axe is dangerous, a dull one doubly so. It is a must to keep the axe sharp. Well, not sharp enough to shave with, but sharp. The best sharpening device is no longer available—progress, again. This was a round stone mounted on a sort of bicycle seat and frame; it revolved by pedal power and was kept wet with a constant supply of dripping water. The old grindstone was perfect for sharpening axes. Electric power makes the stone turn too fast, heating up the axe. Lacking a grindstone, you can use files or various grades of hand-held stone to sharpen your axe. With patience and skill that you have to learn, it is possible to keep a good cutting blade. Inevitably you will nick the blade on hitting hidden wire, spiles, or stones. To touch up a blade in the field I use a relatively new honing device in which industrial diamonds are embedded. It cuts fast and is easy to use.

The axe fell from use as the primary woods tool because its efficient use requires skill and strength. It's easier to use a crosscut saw; it's easier still to use a chainsaw. Also, axes remove a lot of wood in felling a tree or bucking a log—much more than saws do—and this wood is waste, or anyway it usually is. As a final word on the axe, and on the kind of world in which it had a more honored place than it has in our own, I pass on a story about axe chips that I had from an old-timer. He said his folks were poor. Nothing odd about that, but he explained *how* poor. When wood was being chopped in winter someone would come out of the house occasionally with a pan of heated wood chips to put around the feet of the cutters. They had no shoes.

HAND SAWS

To our forefathers who had only axes for tree-felling and cutting big firewood, the two-man crosscut saw must have seemed like manna from heaven. It was a wonderful tool. It still is. It runs for free—no gas to buy. And it's safe—nobody ever cut his nose off with a big old crosscut saw. These saws are still made and available. They're about six feet long, and while an experienced pair of sawyers can saw wood with a crosscut almost as fast as a chainsaw could do the job, you do need a helper to use one. To my mind, the major drawback of a two-man crosscut saw is that sharpening the teeth and setting them at the correct angle for efficient cutting are tricky jobs. Sharpening a crosscut saw is an art, one that I can't claim to have mastered. So I use a chainsaw mostly. Still, I have spent many a pleasant hour to-ing and fro-ing on a sharp two-man saw helping my aged neighbor get in his winter wood supply. Using a two-man saw with a genial com-

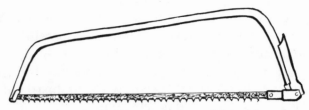

A bow saw or Swedish saw, above, and an old-fashioned two-man crosscut saw, below.

panion is a dandy way to visit, to admire the weather and the view, and to watch the geese flying south.

In addition to the big crosscut saw there is a bewildering array of smaller hand saws to be used for pruning and bucking small wood. Concerning pruning saws I will make an exception to my rule of not recommending specific tools. I am addicted to an axe-handled pruning saw that goes under the name of Meylan. It has a curved blade in two sizes: 15 inch and 18 inch. This blade is mounted on an axe handle, and opposite to the cutting surface there is a hook with which to pull down the branch you have cut should it lodge above you. With the long handle you can stand off and admire your work without putting your eye out by having to be up close to it with a short, one-handed saw. Using two hands also gives you more leverage. In my experience the Meylan saw is a superior tool for pruning softwoods. I can reach up to nine feet with this saw.

One of my neighbors looks down on my favorite, the Meylan. He uses a version of the Swedish pulp or bow saw for pruning. I do not like this sort of saw for pruning. It has a short reach. The frame gets in the way. However, the pulp saw is a handy tool for salvaging small stuff for the stove. Many people waste perfectly good wood because it is not sensible to use a chainsaw on small limb wood. For cutting slender sticks the chainsaw is expensive and dangerous, and it makes hard work. Small branches do not sit calmly while being attacked by a chainsaw. They bounce around and fly off at odd tangents. On the other hand, you power the pulp saw, and your kind of manpower is inexpensive. With a sturdy sawbuck you can cut limbs as small as an inch in diameter with a pulp saw.

A first cousin to the pulp saw is the long-handled pruning saw. This is a much longer critter than the Meylan. It comes with a 16-foot pole, sometimes in one piece and sometimes jointed. The length allows you to prune softwoods to the length of a full log.

In forestry school we learned the Tarzan method of pruning. This involves climbing a white or red pine to the height of 16 feet and then working down, cutting the branches in the whorl above you with a pulp saw and remembering to keep the branch you're holding on to for last. I am sure that today's sophisticated forestry students would sneer at the Tarzan method. Maybe they prune with lasers now.

WEDGES

If you'll be cutting trees more than about eight or ten inches in diameter—either to fell them or to buck them up—you'll need wedges to insert in the cut as you go along. For goodness sake

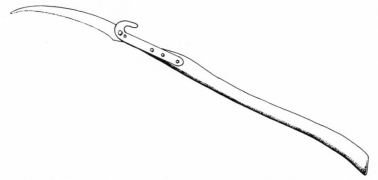

Meylan saw for pruning. The blade is 15 inches long, curved to allow you to apply maximum force when using the saw to prune a high branch. Use the hook below the blade to pull down severed branches. The axe-type handle shown is 34 inches long, though the saw can be fitted onto a 16-foot pole, as well.

don't use steel wedges for this job: they'll wreck your saw if you hit them with it, and you will. I don't like the plastic wedges you can buy in hardware or forestry supply stores. They won't damage your saw, but I find them too slippery, especially when they are cold. I like wooden wedges. You can buy them, or you can make your own of beech, maple, or oak. A good size is 2 inches wide, 1 inch thick at the big end and $1/8$-inch thick at the narrow end, and 6 inches long.

Peavey. The iron hook swings below the iron head on its pivot to engage the tree to be moved. Above, the tool is shown in use, levering a log.

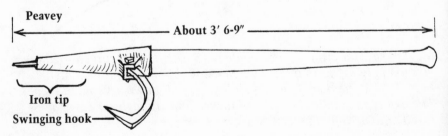

Peavey

About 3' 6-9"

Iron tip
Swinging hook

PEAVEY

This is a logger's specialty tool and emblem of honor. It has a sturdy hardwood handle about 4 feet long with an iron-shod end from which hangs on a pivot or clevis a curved bar that looks (to people my age) for all the world like one half of a pair of ice tongs. You set the point on the end of this bar into a log and then use the handle as a lever to rotate the log. The peavey is the best tool this side of a $50,000 skidder or a good woods horse for moving logs. If you're going to be moving logs more than a little bit, you'll find a peavey useful.

OTHER TREE-MOVERS

Some professional loggers use a system of engine-powered cables to move logs around in and out of woodlots. A spar tree is selected in the cutting area, and as many trees as possible are cut within reach of a grapple which rides on a cable attached to the spar tree on one end and to a power source (usually a tractor) at the other. For the right job in the right place, it is a dandy idea, but it would seldom fit the small woodlot owner's scale. I have seen in operation a similar but much simpler device which I like better. It is experimental and I do not know the price range, but it looks safe, quick, and practical. The operation revolves around a small diesel winch mounted on a sled and equipped with chains for anchoring the sled in place. The sled with its winch can be delivered to a job on an ordinary pickup truck. The sled is anchored in the cutting area. One operator drags the grapple on a cable—maximum length, 200 feet; practical length, 150 feet—to a cut tree. One that is limbed works best. The grapple is fixed and the winch yanks the log to a designated point. It is possible for one man to do the whole job. Two are better. The fancy rig that I watched had a walky-talky to communicate between the winch operator and the cutter. The device is as good as a trained woods horse.

You can adapt the cable-logging principle to a small, largely

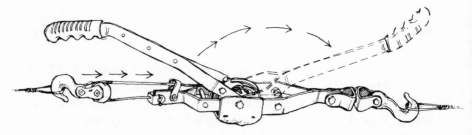

Come-along. A portable, hand-operated winch that can be used to move—slowly—logs, down trees, and other heavy loads in the woods.

muscle-powered operation by investing $50 in a come-along, a hand-operated device of cables, pulleys, ratchets, and stops that allows you to hoist or drag loads far heavier than you could stir by direct application of your strength. The come-along is slow, but, properly set up, it can be used to pull down hung-up trees, and to move logs short distances.

VEHICLES

Back when, I had a caterpillar tractor-bulldozer with a winch to make roads, ponds, and water bars, and to drag logs or firewood or pulp loads with. While I was not as skillful a tractor operator as my neighbor, who boasted that he could peel a grape with a seven-foot bulldozer blade, it was a great life, giving you a massive power complex which had to be curbed constantly for fear of pushing the whole woodlot into the next county.

There is no way that an ordinary woodlot could possibly support the care and feeding of even a small dozer, but maybe a group of woodlot owners could buy one and take turns at using and maintaining it.

I do not recommend the conventional, wheeled farm tractor in the woods. For rough woods work these machines are unstable. They tip over all too easily and can get badly stuck in wet ground. Commercial cutters use an articulated-wheeled tractor—good, but expensive and I think, from observation only, that they do a lot of damage. Maybe I was watching an inept operator or a careless one—there are such.

So how do you get your wood out of the woods? My first venture in this field involved a metal, rubber-tired wheelbarrow. I pushed it into the woods, cut and bucked a tree into appropriate lengths for the stove, and trundled the load to the house. That is a hard way to keep warm, but it is possible, or it was in 1943. About the same time I used another method that involved slave labor, not my own. We had two attractive daughters. Young men flocked. In those far-off days young men had to be polite to older men with talented daughters, so I invited them to manhandle short log lengths to the house where I would cut them into stovewood. Ropes and peaveys were the only available tools. I opine that this sort of exploitation is no longer possible, and in any case not every woodlot owner is blessed with beautiful offspring.

Enough of foolishness. For easy hauling on a trail or path that is without large rocks or stumps, a small, low-slung riding garden tractor—usually 6 to 16 horsepower—with an attached cart works very well. I fell a tree in the home woodlot and buck it into eight-foot lengths. I load these on the little cart and carry the wood to the woodpile, where I cut it into stove lengths for splitting and stacking. I do this to the tune of a cord or so each year. The method is a bit slow, but I am not one to rush.

If one has to haul some distance or over rugged terrain, it is sensible to rent or borrow a four-wheel-drive pickup truck. These machines can safely and well negotiate woods roads providing the ground is fairly dry, frozen, or covered with light snow. A sturdy pickup will carry a good load, but do pay attention to the manufacturer's specifications as to maximum weight. This is a pleasant and relatively easy way to harvest trees from the woodlot, especially if you can shanghai an able companion. Better yet, shanghai several and have a wood-gathering bee in which enough wood is procured for a few households. Getting firewood this way is easy, and I find it a pleasant way to spend a fall afternoon. Even in the Machine Age, many hands make light work.

If you are faced with a fairly large cut of both firewood and lumber, look around for a tractor operator with a conscience, one who will try to avoid young trees, who will minimize bark and root damage, and who will respect wet or steep spots in the wood-

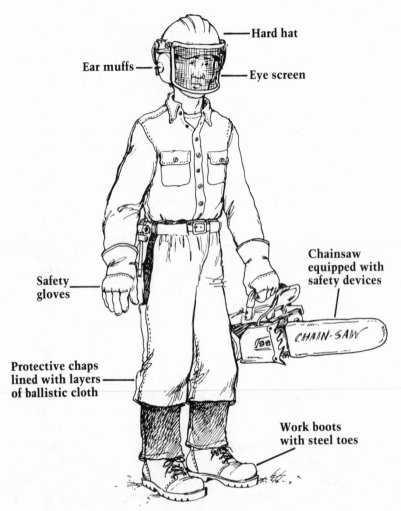

Hard hat

Ear muffs

Eye screen

Chainsaw equipped with safety devices

Safety gloves

CHAIN-SAW

Protective chaps lined with layers of ballistic cloth

Work boots with steel toes

The state of the art in safety clothing for woods work, from steel-capped shoes to extra-tough chaps and trousers, to hard hat with built-in eye- and ear protection.

lot. If such there be, mark him well and ask him to get to roadside trees which you have marked, felled, and limbed. In some parts of the country horses are beginning to make a modest comeback in woods work. If you can find a logger with a woods-trained horse who will hire out the hauling of logs for you, you're in luck. Use him. He'll probably cost less than a heavy-equipment operator, and his animals will do far less damage to your woodlot.

PROTECTIVE CLOTHING

You can do your woodlot work in a bathing suit (not smart); or you can go to a forestry-supply store and outfit yourself with a full suit of protective clothing that will claim to make you proof against any mishap short of a direct hit by a falling oak (smart, no doubt, but costly and probably not practicable for the small woodlot owner). Most woods workers compromise. I wear shoes with steel toe-caps, and I wear ear-protectors when I'm running a chainsaw (their racket is deafening—literally). I don't wear a hard hat, but I should, and so should you. The steel toe-caps protect my feet from partial amputation should axe or saw slip, and the hard hat (would) protect my skull from dead branches that may fall when a tree is being felled (they don't call them widow-makers for nothing).

Any clothing you wear cutting wood ought to be free of flaps, scarves, or any fullness that might get caught in machinery or snagged on trees. A hard-finish cloth is also good, for the same reasons. In winter several separate layers of wool clothing are more comfortable than one heavy garment. Cutting wood is strenuous, and one sweats even in below-zero temperatures. You can disperse this excess heat by taking off your hat, by opening the throat of your wool shirt, or by discarding layers of clothing.

CHAINSAWS

I saved the most important woods tool for last. Today a woodsman would no more try to do his work without a chainsaw than a sharp accountant would try to fiddle a favorite client's tax return without an electronic calculator.

My first chainsaw—circa 1946—weighed fifty pounds and had a carburetor which frequently developed the chainsaw engine's equivalent of asthma, requiring much tinkering. The machines have improved a lot since then: they're lighter and safer, and they run better. Chainsaws today come in almost every conceivable size, shape, and weight with different length blades and horsepower. The key for safe and sure operation is maintenance. If you are a good mechanic, swell. Not me. I can comprehend and use machines successfully, but they are not soul mates, and I have no patience with their occasional foibles; and foibles they will have.

My experience with chainsaws has led me to the conclusion that my own safety and happiness depend on a competent and honest chainsaw service man. Find one who gets a lot of business

Chainsaw. The drawing shows a saw of the newest type with many safety devices not found on older saws.

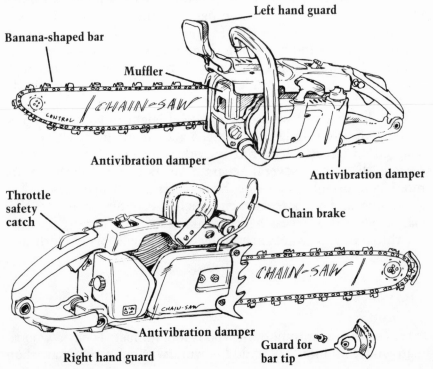

and has a good reputation in your locale. Explain to this paragon what sort of work you plan to do and where your woodlot is. Take his advice on length of blade and power. If he's a dealer (he probably is), buy the kind of saw he sells. Return the machine to him for frequent service checks if you are a heavy user of the machine. Happiness is a well-sharpened chain, a well-serviced engine, and a full tank of fuel.

Carefully nurtured, these machines last a long time. I have a large, long-bladed monster over twenty years old and still humming. I have another, smaller machine which is cutting well at ten years of age. I bought them at the same place. The best chainsaw dealer is the blood brother of the machines he sells. It pays to stick with such a person rather than shopping around for price. You will be safer, and the machine will last longer, snarling happily all the while.

You *can* sharpen chainsaw chains yourself. There are a number of mechanical aids. I did it for years. Unless you like that sort of work, however, I recommend returning the saw to the shop for sharpening. The shops have equipment that makes a more uniform and better job possible. Do not hesitate, however, to carry a chainsaw file and touch up the blade occasionally in the field. No matter how careful or expert you are, you will from time to time hit a sugar spout, a nail, or a bit of barbed wire hidden in the growing tree. Nicks so caused can be smoothed out quite handily.

Chainsaws are always dangerous. Be vigilant. The machine must be treated with the utmost respect. Think of a running chainsaw as a loaded, cocked gun. Don't run a saw when you're tired. Don't run one when you're off balance. You can fall on the saw. Beware of chainsaw kickback. Saws kick back most easily when the tip of the running saw encounters wood or other material that causes the force of the moving chain momentarily to be translated into a sudden up or down jerk rather than its being directed to drive the chain around its track. When this happens, unless you have the saw firmly in control, it can rebound from whatever it has hit and bite you. Never saw one-handed. If you must raise the saw to cut at a level above your knees, be extra careful. The engine of a medium-sized saw runs at about 8,000 rpm. At that speed the saw can injure you seriously before you know what has happened.

I'm not going to recommend makes, sizes, or styles of chainsaw. Don't start out with a saw that is so big and powerful that you're not confident you can operate it with full control; but stay away from the new "minisaws" and featherweight models, too. The smallest chainsaws are too light. They chatter; they won't stay in the cut. They may be underpowered, too, leading you to bear down on the saw as you cut to make the cut go faster. All these conditions are potentially dangerous. In picking out a first chainsaw, be guided by your conscientious dealer. And when you start to work, go slow. Be careful.

TREE FELLING

Now that the tools of the woodlot worker are assembled and described, what do you do with them? Please do not get your hopes up. I am not going to give you such detailed instructions that you can leap out into your woods and become an instant expert woodsman. The proper and efficient use of the tools described in the last few pages requires patience and practice. It also requires care. You have to learn by doing. There are, however, a few ironclad rules, most of them having to do with safety.

1. The axe and the chainsaw chain must be sharp. The axe head must seat firmly on the handle.
2. Keep people and pets out of the work area—keep a twenty-foot leeway at least. When felling trees, keep spectators further away still.
3. Remove any obstructions to the sides or overhead which might deflect an axe blow.
4. Do not use bifocals in axe or chainsaw work. There is a troublesome small blind spot.
5. Aim every axe stroke carefully, as if trying for a hole-in-one. Your foot is at stake, not merely the score.
6. If you absolutely must cut with saw or axe above the level of your knees choke up on the axe handle, making for a short and controlled grip.

7. When limbing, try to put something between yourself and the cutting tool you're using.
8. Stance is important: firm base, legs apart, watch for icy spots, loose stones, or branches that can trip.
9. Take a breather from time to time to rest and survey progress.
10. Select and clear an escape route from a tree to be felled.
11. Remember that chainsaws can cut either up or down.
12. Inspect every tree you plan to fell very carefully for dead branches, diseased spots, decided lean, signs of metal in the wood, footing in the work area.

In felling a tree you want, first of all, to get the tree to fall in the clear and not to hang up in the branches of trees around it. Therefore begin cutting trees at the edge of the woodlot, along a path or in a natural forest opening, so there will be a clear area for them to fall into. The first tree cut will help make way for succeeding trees to fall in the clear.

Tree felling is the trickiest job in the woods. Don't charge right in; rather, carefully size up the tree you want to fell before you set to work. Trees on the edge of an opening tend to fall into the opening, and trees on a side hill tend to fall downhill. Look your tree over from several angles. Does it have a pronounced lean, or "sweep"? If so, it will be difficult or impossible to get it to fall in a direction different from the direction of its lean. Does the tree have large branches on one side and not on others? The weight of the branches will pull the tree so it will fall toward the side where the branches are. What's the weather? A sudden puff of wind can affect tree felling. A tree in full leaf can act like a sail, and when it's partially cut through the wind can make it fall unpredictably. How's the tree's health? Dead and rotten spots in the trunk can influence how the tree will fall. What about other nearby trees? Are there trees that will obstruct the fall of your tree, or that will catch it and hang it up?

You have picked a tree for your first cut. Before doing anything else, decide on your escape route. If necessary, clear this path of obstructions. It is hard to outrun a falling tree, so it is sensible to find a sound tree nearby to get behind if worst comes to worst. Even if the tree you're felling falls exactly where you hoped it would, get away from it as it falls. The severed butt of the tree—

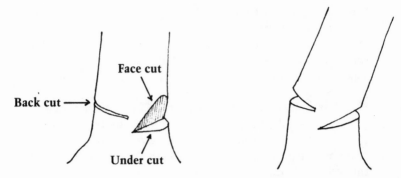

Back cut →

Face cut

Under cut

Face cut allows tree to tip

Felling a tree. The drawing at left shows the wedge-shaped face cut on the side the tree is to fall toward, with the back cut approaching it; the right-hand drawing shows how the face cut allows the tree to fall forward.

where you cut it through—can twist, jump, and thrash about as the tree falls. If it jumps on you, you have big trouble.

To fell a tree, you make a flat undercut on the side toward which you wish to have the tree fall and then you make a diagonal cut from above to connect with the first cut. A wedge of wood will fall out. If you have not been careful in cutting out the wedge, you may have to dislodge it with your axe. The wedge or "face cut" should be as shallow as possible—never more than a third of the way through the trunk. When the undercut is complete and the wedge is removed, you make a back cut, on the opposite side of the tree an inch or so above the level of the undercut. As the back cut approaches the undercut, the tree falls.

Both undercuts and back cuts should be flat, and they should be parallel. I sometimes have trouble achieving this. In my case I think that the difficulty is faulty eyesight, and so I take the chicken route if there are no professionals nearby to scoff. I carry a lumber-marking crayon in my pocket. On the bark I mark the flat and diagonal undercut; then I mark the back cut. This gives me a sort of template to guide my cutting. Pros would scream with laughter at this sissy way of doing things, but I really do not care. I would rather do the job well by whatever timid means than botch it by trying to pretend to be better than I am.

Begin with a small tree—four to six inches in diameter. This is good practice, and a mistake is not fatal. Make the undercut an inch or so deep on the side of the trunk facing where you expect the tree to fall. Make the downward diagonal cut to meet this depth. Go around to the opposite side of the tree and start the back cut, parallel and an inch or two above the bottom of the undercut. Do not rush. Stop and take a look to make sure that all is proceeding according to plan. A slight cracking noise and a tremble in the tree will signal that the tree is about to fall. Withdraw your saw and get away. Mostly the tree falls over without fuss just where you have planned.

Sometimes even a small tree is reluctant to drop. Quite often when I am making the back cut, I let the saw idle and lean my shoulder against the trunk near the end of the cut and apply pressure. This makes it easy for the tree to make up its mind to fall. If you have a helper, this person could place the sharp end of a peavey on the trunk as high as he can reach and, at the crucial moment, give a push.

These ploys only work on small stuff. For bigger trees the proper undercut and back cut well applied are usually enough to send the tree crashing just where you wanted it to go. For big trees which look as though they might be cranky, one or more wooden wedges placed in the back cut, behind the saw, and tapped in gently with the poll of the axe from time to time will direct the fall and will provide a safety measure against having the tree tip backward, closing the back cut and trapping the saw. You insert the wedge when the cut is deep enough to hold both wedge and saw. Let the saw idle in the cut, tap in the wedge, take

Two wedges in a big tree

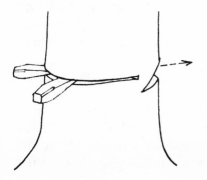

Felling wedges, driven into the back cut behind the advancing saw, assist the tree's correct fall and prevent the tree from seizing the saw in the cut.

the saw and deepen the cut a little, stop, tap in the wedge in further, proceed. Keep the saw a mite ahead of the wedge. You may nick the wedge. No matter—that's why you're using a wooden wedge.

I must admit that I am daunted by the problem of trying to fell a tree uphill. Trees usually do not want to fall that way, and gravity is against the project. Cutting to fell a tree uphill can be done by the expert with an accurate undercut and back cut and with the prompt and judicious use of wedges. There are two good ways to get around this problem. One is to have a tractor pull the tree as you cut, to make the tree fall uphill. The other is to see if you cannot plan your work so it is safe and practical to let the tree fall downhill, where it wants to go anyway.

There are some little but useful tips in felling trees. To check the accuracy of the undercut, you can place the head of your axe firmly against the base of the undercut. The axe handle will point almost precisely to where the tree will fall. Before finishing the back cut it is wise to make sure the hinge—the diminishing section of wood between the undercut and the back cut—is developing evenly. For this it is helpful (but not essential) to have a companion in crime. You can develop a set of signals to indicate that the hinge is not developing evenly. Sometimes the hinge is hard to judge when the tree is large. You cannot see around the tree, and you may not know that you are cutting too deeply on one side or the other, making a back cut that is not exactly parallel to the undercut. The helper can take over the job of tapping the wedges as you cut. He can tell you that the top of the tree is beginning to quiver so that you both can be prepared to take your escape routes.

When there is the slightest doubt about the success of a felling operation, save yourself—leave the saw behind. Saws are not naturally replaceable as people are, but a new saw bar is a lot cheaper than a hospital visit or a funeral.

Here in the east not many woodlot workers are faced with a tree that is much thicker than the bar of their saw is long. To meet this situation, however, there is a simple technique called boxing. You make two side-by-side cuts on each side of the tree. The combined depth of the cuts depends on the size of the tree and the depth of your saw bar. When you have made the cuts, remove the wood between them. The effect, of course, is that of making the tree narrow enough so that you can use your saw in the ordinary way to make the undercut and the back cut.

If you're a beginner, the best time to exercise caution in felling a tree is before you start. Begin with small trees. Look and think hard before you start to cut. Don't take on a tree unless you're sure you have it sized up and are confident you can bring it all the way down safely.

Sooner or later (probably sooner, if you're working in a wood-lot) a tree you cut will not fall completely down but will hang up in nearby trees—a frustrating and dangerous impasse. What do you do? To begin with, be extra careful. The hung-up tree can fall

The author holds an axe in the face cut of a tree to be felled. The axe handle indicates the direction in which the tree will fall.

Freeing a hung-up tree. Use a peavey at the tree's butt to twist it out of the tree it is stuck in; or, as at right, get a lever (the peavey will serve here, too) under the butt and lift the tree, allowing it to move backward and so to fall free.

at any time. It can fall on you. Don't pass beneath it. Don't let anybody else near it.

First comes a careful inspection. Can you weaken the hinge a little with axe or saw, carefully? Will another wedge do the trick? Maybe a branch of your tree is caught on that of a neighboring tree. Maybe you can twist the trunk—the hinge having been cut through—with the peavey. Gravity will help here. The tree wants to fall away from entanglement. It may be possible, using a stout pole or the peavey again, to lift and pry the trunk so that it slides off the stump or backs away clear of the tree it's stuck in. Even an inch or so may help, and this trick can be used several times until the tree settles to the ground.

If none of these easy tricks works, and if you're harvesting the hung-up tree for cordwood and not for any purpose requiring an intact log, you can cut short sections off the butt of the stuck tree, which has the same effect as prying the butt. Everybody uses this method of freeing hung-up trees. I use it. And yet I would hate to be guilty of advocating it. It is foolhardy in many ways. The tree can fall on you. You can get the saw stuck in the trunk. You often have to cut at shoulder height to make this method work. The severed butt can land on your shin or foot.

If you must cut sections of trunk to release a hung-up tree, be especially careful. Cut the hung-up trunk from the underside up with the top of your chainsaw bar. If you cut from the top of the log down in the normal way, the cut will close on your saw when you've gone part way through, and you won't be able to pull the saw free. When the butt is cut through it will fall down and backward. Be sure your saw and feet are well out of the way.

There are other ways to free hung-up trees. The best way, which may not be open to you, is to winch the trunk down with a tractor-mounted winch or by using a come-along. If you do not have the equipment for the winch job, you might consider felling the tree on which your tree is hung. Maybe you wanted to cut that one anyway, so this is a reasonable solution. You do have to take care with your escape route, though, because you now have to watch *two* trees fall, possibly in different directions. Do not be addle-pated enough to try to climb your tree to cut the trapped branches, or to try to climb the tree yours is hung up in. Such an attempt is tedious, ineffective, and super-dangerous.

When a hung-up tree does fall, it may bounce around some in ways that are difficult to anticipate. This is not usual, but you should be aware that it can happen so you and any helpers can get out of the way.

LIMBING AND BUCKING

At last, you have the tree down. It must be limbed.

It is natural, perhaps, to relax once the big felling operation is over. Don't. Limbing has its own set of special hazards, the chief of which is in the form of branches under tension that act like springs. These are usually branches on the underside of the fallen tree or those which have been pressed against a rock or other tree.

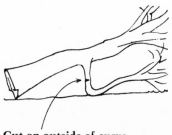

A sprung limb. The limb in the drawing bears part of the weight of the fallen tree and thus is under tension. When cut, it may snap back. Cut limbs like these slowly and carefully, close to the trunk, from the outside of their curves.

Cut on outside of curve

When branches under tension are cut, they often spring back or whip around. They may even permit the whole trunk to settle suddenly to the ground or to either side. The whole tree is sort of like the old-fashioned deadfall trap with which I used to catch skunks for my mother's proposed neckpiece. Only, in this case, you might be the skunk.

The problem is not without several good solutions. Before limbing, it might be possible to relieve the tension on branches by twisting the trunk with the peavey. If this is not practicable, cut branches under tension slowly and carefully. The idea is to weaken the branch gradually so it eases apart instead of snapping. Start limbing at the lower branches. The lay of the land may require limbing from the top, but this way you are always fighting the tops of the uncut branches. This is a last-resort approach.

I like to cut a few branches, pull them out of the way, and stack them nearby so they won't have to be handled over and over again. It is a good plan to make a clean work space by putting aside branches as you move along the trunk. Now I realize that this is not the way professional cutters work. They are under time pressure. They cut the branches in the same way I've advised, but they seldom stack them to the side. Cutting a few branches and stacking them to one side to make a clear work space is slower and safer, however, and as a friend of mine says, "What's time to a hen?"

Piling branches neatly to one side as you limb is also a safety measure. A tangle of branches makes footing tricky when you are engaged in limbing a tree. You would not enjoy stumbling with a sharp axe or a snarling chainsaw in your grip.

It is not always possible, but try to put the tree trunk or a fat branch between you and the limb you are cutting. This is your bulwark against a slip of axe or saw. In practice it means that you are frequently cutting the branches on the opposite side of the tree from the side on which you are standing.

Many woodsmen use only the chainsaw for limbing. I like to use both axe and chainsaw—not one in each hand, though. Small branches suit the axe. Cut them with the grain of the wood, not against it. Larger branches are for the chainsaw. I think that this is an easy way to work. It provides variety and gives some relief from the quite horrendous racket of the chainsaw.

The author uses his axe to clear small limbs from a felled tree.

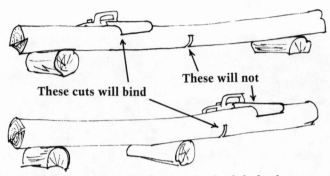

These cuts will bind

These will not

Bucking a down tree for logs or firewood. The labels show cuts that will seize or bind the saw as the weight of unsupported portions of the log closes the saw cut.

Using the axe to limb, and taking time to stack cut branches to the side, give me a chance to turn off the chainsaw from time to time. Do not let it idle unattended. The saw cut off, silence reigns. I can take a breather and see what lies ahead. Incidentally, when you restart the saw, don't be macho about it. Put the saw on a firm base—a stump, a down tree trunk, or the ground. The big boys like to show off by holding the saw in one hand and starting it with the other in a dashing rip. Nix. This may save seconds, but it is dangerous.

In cutting large branches into sections for stovewood, and in bucking the tree trunk itself if it's destined for cordwood rather than for lumber, you need to be alert to avoid pinching or binding the saw. I touched on this in describing how to bring down a hung-up tree. The problem is one of weight distribution. If a tree trunk, log, or heavy branch is supported at both ends, and you cut through it from the top down, then as your cut progresses the severed ends of the log will fall together, closing the cut and pinching your saw. The answer is to cut from the underside up, or to use wedges. Cut straight down until you can insert a wooden wedge. As the cut proceeds, the wedge is tapped into the cut. When the cut tries to close, the wedge keeps it from pinching the saw. This makes it possible to cut a large tree all the way through with a minimum of trouble. Some cutters cut down for a bit, then shift the saw so that it cuts far into the opposite side of the log from where they are standing, letting the saw undercut a bit on that side. Before the saw binds, it is removed, and the cutter uses the top of the saw to cut up to meet the previous cut. It takes practice and judgment to withdraw the saw at the right moment. Naturally, if the end of the trunk or branch you want to buck is unsupported or lies on deep snow, there is no problem. Cut all the way through from the top with abandon.

I do not pretend that these hints are all you need to know. Felling and limbing trees is an art form not learned in one easy lesson. Success comes from practice, feel, and intuition, all learned by trial and error. I hope, however, that I have at least given you the conviction that in approaching woods work you must go slowly, thoughtfully, and carefully. The trial-and-error you will learn by will necessarily be largely error at first. Take care that the errors be not injurious or fatal.

VI | 🌲🌲

From Seedling
to Harvest

IN MANAGING WOODLANDS for yield of forest products man is up against the fact that nature takes much more time over trees than she does over radishes, or over men. I have said that it takes sixty to a hundred years to grow a prime hardwood tree—almost that long for a conifer. This is the life of a man, or longer. Production forestry, therefore, has time as its final adversary; its aim is to *speed up* the growth of valuable timber. Large commercial forest industries do this by massive harvests and replantings, by maximum mechanization of all stages in the work, and by spraying. There is much waste, and much damage to fragile biological systems in these practices. In a small woodlot, I hope, the owner will eschew such steamroller tactics and will use other, less drastic measures to manage his woods for the best yield of marketable timber and other products.

In the woodlot, I, too, am trying to speed the trees up, to encourage the fast, healthy growth of the most valuable species. But I aim to do this by managing the access of light into my woodlot, and by reducing the number of trees per acre to the point where the largest possible number of crop trees fulfill their potential for growth without inhibiting each other through competition for light, water, and soil nutrients. This is the method of the approach to forestry that I called in Chapter IV "intensive woodlot forestry," an approach the goal of which is a woodlot that yields a variety of forest products fairly continuously, each product having a use.

I have discussed some of the implications and techniques of intensive woodlot forestry in earlier chapters, chiefly from the point of view of hardwood forests. This was because the reader whose lapel I most want to grab onto is, I figure, a novice or would-be forester and not a veteran. His little woods are made up of trees he did not plant, trees nobody planted; and over most of North America it follows that his woods are often hardwoods. The trees in such a woodlot are "givens," and their management consists for the most part of culling runts and damaged and malformed specimens for fuel wood, particle board, or pulpwood so as to open up the stand enough to encourage the better trees but not so much as to make the trees sprout from the trunks—as hardwoods will when they're overthinned. If, after inferior trees have been thinned, a hardwood stand is still too tight, it may be time, with a forester's advice, to contract for a selective timber harvest. Although there is plenty of work in managing hardwoods, the planning it involves is mainly a matter of caring for trees that are already there, and therefore the whole enterprise of hardwood management may seem pretty passive, at least in comparison with management of softwoods. With the latter, once you get started, you'll often be working with trees you planted.

Again, the aim is helping nature along, speeding her up. Over most of the country that supports woodlots there is no such thing as untended open land. Open land becomes woods. Open land is Stage 1 in the forest succession. But the process is slow. In fields, in burned-over land going back to woods, nature may take a hundred years or so to act out the complete drama of weeds, shrubs of many kinds, light-seeded invading "pioneer" trees which act as nurse crops for the succeeding forest trees. I won't live that long, and as an intensive woodlot manager I am impatient to see results more promptly. Therefore I plant trees.

Before an abandoned field gets too cluttered with shrubs and small pioneer trees I take a hand. I plant softwoods. Even though many parts of the northeast are naturally hardwood land, it is not sensible to plant hardwoods. The tree nurseries do not usually supply hardwood seedlings. These are difficult to grow and difficult to dig and plant. So even in hardwood lands I plant red or white pines; various spruces; and balsam for Christmas trees, maybe Scotch pine for this purpose, too.

I try not to provide a mini-monoculture—a banquet for the pests and diseases which afflict a certain kind of tree. I plant several different species in blocks, remembering that a healthy woodlot—whether planted by nature or by me—is diverse and various in the species it supports. An acre of pine, say, is not as appealing to beetles that dote on pine as ten acres might be, so I plant an acre of white pine. The acre next door might be spruce or red pine. The next block could be larch or, if you are aiming at Christmas trees, it could be balsam or Scotch pine. The point is to thwart disease and insects which tend to specialize in a particular evergreen species.

TREE PLANTING

Before putting in an order for seedlings from a state or a private commercial nursery, decide what you want to plant in any particular area. You will, of course, be guided by the quality of the site. If you have a wet, north-facing slope, hemlock could be the answer. Not many people plant that tree. Most lumber mills may have some hemlock for sale as rough planks or boards or as dimensional stock (two-by-fours and the like), but the wood is not highly regarded. Larch is another softwood that is seldom planted but that will grow almost anywhere. It prefers damp terrain.

In most sites you'll do best to plant pines or spruces. White pine can stand quite a wet site—not swampy, but moist. It can also do well in sandy loam. Red pine is a bit more fussy. It likes a well-drained site but not bone dry or ledgy. The spruces tend to be quite catholic in their tastes, but they do not like to have their feet wet. Red spruce has a peculiar affinity for white birch. One often sees these two intermingled. Red cedar—really a juniper and usually not available as seedlings—has a fine aromatic wood used for specialties and also for posts and other applications where the wood comes into contact with the ground. It is moisture-resistant. Look at your planting space and decide—perhaps after consulting a forester—which type of tree will do best. And so place your seedling order.

The seedlings arrive. If you cannot plant at once—a day or so doesn't matter—you should make a shallow trench in a shady place, break open the bundles the seedlings are shipped in, and spread the seedlings as evenly as possible in the trench, immediately covering the roots with damp soil. Don't let the roots dry out. The main cause of seedling mortality is dry roots. It would do no harm to water the trees well each day until planting time.

If you think big and have a large, relatively flat area free of stumps and rocks for your plantation, you may want to hire a tree-planting machine with a trained crew to do the job. I think that small is beautiful, however, and, over the years, I have planted some 30,000 evergreen seedlings by hand. Usually I planted 2,000 to 5,000 seedlings each spring.

You do it this way. First, go to where you have heeled in the seedlings. Pick up about fifty at a time and immediately immerse the roots in a bucket half filled with muddy water so as to keep them moist. Carry the bucket of seedlings to the planting site. For future ease of tending the trees, make sure that the first row you plant is straight and subsequent rows are parallel to it. It may sound silly and nasty neat, but I actually put down a garden line for the first row.

There are a number of ways to plant seedlings, and several special planting tools. If this was an ideal world where everything was done the very best way, one would carefully dig a hole twice as large as necessary. One would spread the roots of the seedlings to be planted, place them in the hole, then fill in the soil, making sure that there were no air pockets. One would leave a small depression to collect water, and there would be a tiny earth dam to contain the water which would be put on the seedlings daily for the first week after planting. Alas, this is not a perfect world, and having several thousand seedlings to plant precludes any such ideal of meticulousness.

What, then, is a workable method? Some people use a mattock. Swing the mattock to remove a scalp of turf. Swing it again to make a little hole. Stick the roots into that hole; pull soil over the roots and tamp with the feet. This is a good method, and most country places possess a mattock.

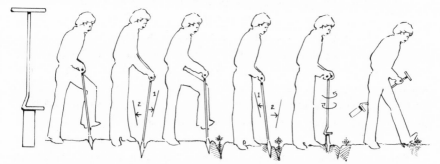

Planting seedlings. The drawing shows the use of a special tree-planting spade, but any narrow spade can be used the same way.

I use a light spade. This particular spade is made of very good steel and is called a lady's English spade. The steel has to be good because every time you plant a seedling with this tool, the blade will flex. Push the spade into the ground at a slight angle. Bend it forward to make a V to receive the seedling roots. Pop the roots into the opening, step forward, and stamp the V closed with your heel. Sounds tedious. It really is not. You can plant one seedling a minute with a high rate of survival this way, providing you take some precautions.

You are ready to put in the first seedling, but what spacing? I plant white pine on four-foot centers (that is, each tree is the center of a circle with a four-foot radius). This is twice as many trees as will grow on the site. I have a reason. I have discovered that the shoot borer (or white pine weevil) and the white pine blister rust are both inhibited by shade. The borer destroys the leader shoot, making the tree stag-headed, and the blister girdles the tree and kills it. Getting these troubles under some control by shading them out has worked for me. The tight spacing allows the side branches of seedlings to grow together quite quickly, shading the ground. Currants and gooseberries, which are hosts of the white pine blister, have trouble getting started in the shade. The shoot borer pupae are kept from early emergence, because the ground is shaded and cold. When they do emerge, the pine leader is ahead of them and safe from damage.

Most of the other evergreens can be planted on six-foot centers. I have found that red pine will do well on eight-foot centers. The wider spacing saves on seedlings, and it spares the back if you are using the spade method of planting.

One more tip on planting is that seedlings should not be planted deeper than the depth at which they grew in the nursery. When you look carefully at the root system of a seedling you will notice a root collar, which was the mark of the seedling's depth at the nursery. When inserting the seedling into its slot or hole, do not plant deeper than the collar. Doing so can kill the seedling.

You have now completed the year's planting of seedlings. Granted a reasonable rainfall there is no need to water the seedlings. Mowing between the rows is a nice idea, but the seedlings are so small, usually, that there is a good chance some will be mowed down. It is better to forget the newly planted trees for several years. If you have chosen well—tree type, soil, and weather exposure—the seedlings will thrive and a survival of better than 80 per cent is expected. It may be that you will want to replant here and there if the catch has failed.

PRUNING

Rather than worry about seedlings you have just planted, you might put your time to better use by going to a previous planting and looking it over to see if it is time to do some pruning. Softwoods are pruned for a number of reasons (do not prune hardwoods: they sprout where branches were pruned, and so undo your efforts), the chief of which is that when an evergreen branch is removed all the wood the tree makes after the pruning at that spot will be knot-free, and knot-free lumber commands a premium anywhere, anytime. In addition, pruning facilitates working in a softwood plantation. You will return to your plantations again and again in the years to come. It is easier and safer to do maintenance work if the trees are pruned. Dead snags can tear at your clothing, and at your eyes and hide. Finally, dead or shaded branches do not add to tree growth. They may even slow down overall growth. Therefore it makes sense to prune these branches.

I prune every tree in my plantations. Some people only prune what they conceive to be crop trees. I prune them all because I'm aiming at the ideal of intensive woodlot forestry: I expect to use every tree I plant, one way or another. Except for Christmas tree stock in the earliest stages of a plantation, the branches have to come off every tree that is cut and put to use. I submit that it is easier to take branches off when they are relatively small and to do this job piecemeal than it is to limb scores of big, tough branches all at once when the tree is felled. Pruning every tree in a plantation does pay, at least in our form of intensive woodlot forestry.

You might not think that pruning is much by way of entertainment. Not so. Elizabeth finds pruning addictive. It is just as compulsive as peanuts at a cocktail party. I have to watch Elizabeth so that some branches, at least, escape her zeal.

Like any other discipline, pruning has its own set of tools, rules, and procedures. First off, never prune with an axe. It is almost impossible to avoid damaging the adjacent bark. It is also next to impossible to make a clean cut with an axe. Some axe cuts will leave a snag or a hole, and this translates into an imperfection in lumber: evergreens fill any hole with sap, and this becomes a tar pocket in a board. So, no axe pruning.

Commercially speaking, the care we take over pruning is silly, I suppose. When the plantation is old enough for the lower branches to start meeting, we do a little pruning—one or two whorls of branches. Quite often, this can be done easily and quickly with a pair of hand clippers. As in all pruning for any purpose, make a clean cut close to the trunk but without damaging the bark. When it is not practicable to use the clippers, take to the trusty Meylan pruning saw, already touted as a valuable tool.

With all this pruning the ground is being littered with a lot of branches. Many just let them fall, but not I, and again I have my reasons. If you do not dispose in some sensible way of the cut branches, they will trip you up and be a big bother for future pruning or harvesting. I pile pruned branches. Done at the time of cutting, this is not an onerous chore. Let us suppose that you have just cut a branch of a pine. Place this in the row to your right. Maybe to your left, if you are a southpaw. If you keep the butts all in one direction, the pile will be flatter and will rot down more quickly. The branch pile will block one aisle, but the one

The use of the pruning saw for removing high softwood branches.

you are working in will be free for walking and any future work you might do. I take care that cut branches do not touch living wood. It is all too easy for decay mechanisms of all kinds to migrate from dead branches to living wood if the two are in contact.

The best reason for piling pruned branches in orderly rows is that the practice promotes water retention in the plantation. Depending on slope and exposure, snow may drift through and away from a plantation and its melt water be lost to the trees. It would be nice to cause snow to drift within the plantation and to delay the spring melt-off. Such a scheme might increase the water available for the trees by keeping it inside and might also slow down both melt and run-off. I accomplish these very objectives by piling cut branches across the slope of a softwood plantation and, if possible, across the path of the prevailing winter wind. The piled branches act as a snow fence, collecting snow in drifts behind the pile, which is, naturally, continuous because I've been adding branches to the pile as I've moved along pruning through the plantation. The piles tend to prevent rapid melting, thus holding the water longer. They act as a sort of leaky dam, preventing rapid run-off and so protecting against erosion on steep slopes. Too, birds use the branch piles for nesting, and small mammals and birds use them as travel lanes and for protection from predators.

Obviously in a large commercial softwood plantation nobody is going to take the time to pile pruned branches or, for that matter, to prune branches in the first place—but in our kind of forestry doing so is practical, it's easy, and I have found it to be a fine idea.

When to prune, and how much? These are subjective judgments. Pruning is not an exact science: shade, species, site quality, and so on are variables. Elizabeth and I have actually pruned some pine at a very early stage—five years old or so—on our hands and knees with hand clippers, removing a couple of whorls. The branches had to come off sometime. They were not producing. It really was the easiest way for fast-growing young stock on a good site. In other circumstances it might have been a poor use of our time. When to prune rests firmly on your particular situation, then, and on your time and energy.

How much to prune is another question for which there is no short answer. The needles of evergreens are the manufacturing units which make food by which the tree grows. Cutting live branches, unless they are shaded, reduces the number of manufacturing units and so might slow growth. The first move, then, is to cut the dead branches, as many as your strength and reach will permit. The next is to visualize a tree as a pyramid of branches holding up the manufacturing units, leaves or needles. Are the lower branches heavily shaded? Such branches often look dull and dispirited. These are not pulling their weight and may be using energy which can better go to the working branches above. These branches can come off. Under some conditions it is all right to cut some live and unshaded branches when these are in the way or when you wish to prune to a certain height limit for convenience and to produce knot-free wood. In making this judgment, take care. It might be better to leave live branches for a later pruning spree. A rough rule of thumb might be that you never prune more than a total of 25 percent of the tree pyramid at any growth stage.

THINNING

Having pruned your young softwood stand, take a stroll through some of the aisles that you have left clear. Look up. Not many large animals look up. For most, danger does not come from above. On the contrary, you might stub your toe. Take a chance and look up. If the shade is very dense, if the branches above you are beginning to interlace, it means that no tree is getting all the sunlight that it needs to grow evenly and rapidly. You may even notice that the space between the whorls is shortening. Evergreens normally make a whorl of branches at each annual growth point. A persistent shortening of this distance indicates slower growth. This could be caused by drought, but it is likely that slow growth is caused by intense competition. Each acre of forest possesses a limited amount of available light, water, and soil nutrients. This growth material will be used by a thousand stems on an acre, or by two hundred. If growth is slow in a dense softwood stand, overcrowding is probably the reason. Thinning is the answer. Elizabeth and I once had some twenty- to thirty-year-old red spruce, shaded by tall, inferior hardwoods. The spruce were only about five feet tall—silly to thin, but when these trees were thinned their established root systems allowed them to shoot skyward with growth in excess of a foot a year, in spite of the shading hardwoods.

There is a quick-and-dirty way to do thinning called row thinning. A woodlot owner cuts every other row or maybe every third row, completely. Sometimes, there is no salvage. Sometimes the cut trees can be sold for pulp or for log buildings.

Row thinning, when it is done by an adept, is fun to watch. The operator cuts a number of trees in a row part way through. All the crowded side branches tend to keep the trees from falling. At the end of the row the operator cuts one tree so that it falls against its partially cut neighbor. It's the domino theory in action. Although it's a neat trick, however, row thinning is not for the careful woodlot owner or forester. It is wasteful of forest capital. It may cause sun scald and wind throw by making too large an opening in the stand. It does not address itself to crowding in the remaining rows.

I think that thinning ought to be selective: remove runts, malformed or diseased trees in the first step of thinning. Look again at the stand. It may still be too dense. Perhaps there are codominants, so-called, which could be taken out to free a dominant in a favored position. A dominant is a bigger, better, healthier tree on a favorable site, and codominants are similar trees nearby in competition with it. The dominant you release should be a crop tree destined for big things: veneer wood, knotless lumber, or piling.

Very early in the life of a plantation some small trees can be thinned if it is observed that the survival has been good and that there are more trees than will be needed at any stage. Very small, bushy trees can be dug and potted for table Christmas trees. I have done this. Some, especially the spruces, balsam, and Scotch pine, can serve as Christmas trees even when they're up to twenty feet tall; the top part of the tree usually is in good enough form for this purpose. All along, the pruned branches can serve as Christmas greens in season. This sort of casual sale won't pay

A crowded stand of red pines at the Hawk's Hill Demonstration Woodlot.

much, but it does make a worthy contribution to the overall income derived from a woodlot.

A second thinning in softwoods can yield larger logs. I have used thinnings from ten-year-old pines for fence posts. The log should be not less than three inches in diameter at the top of the post-to-be, and it should be nine feet long if the fence is to be horse high and hog tight. Everybody knows that except for red and white cedar, evergreens hardly last one season in contact with the earth, but I have some white and red pine fence posts that are already twenty years on duty. The trick is treating the posts against rot. If there is a treatment plant in your area that applies a vacuum and then preservative under pressure, you are in luck. Otherwise you can treat small batches of posts in an oil barrel with almost any preservative except cuprinol. Porcupines dote on the copper salts.

Successive thinnings will be of more substantial stems yet, suitable for highway guard rails (treated), or pole buildings, or log buildings. The timing and extent of each of these thinnings are decided on by the same judgments. The stand is getting crowded; growth is slowing; it is time to thin.

Starting with some thousand seedlings per acre, you will eventually arrive at about two hundred crop trees well spaced and still growing fast. Of course, this is an ideal, but one can dream. These last, best trees will eventually make a harvest for dimension lumber and boards, and for veneer.

HARVEST

To the point of the first real harvest, I think that going it alone with your own energy and imagination is the way to proceed. I do not think that the average do-it-yourselfer needs much professional advice up to this moment. When you have good, mature trees to sell, however, you should hire a professional forester to oversee the cutting and the sale. Some commercial cutters have larceny in their hearts. Some lumber mills have a penchant for being greedy at your cost. The forester—as suggested in Chapter IV—should be your man. He should act in your interest, and in the interests of your woodlot's good health.

Even the best foresters sometimes become case-hardened to things that I think are important: avoiding wet spots in woods work, protecting young trees, preventing soil compaction and erosion. Some of them have even fallen for the blandishments of those who sell chemicals—to kill culls instead of turning them into firewood, to kill bugs, to poison predators, and so on. Find a forester who knows enough to avoid such practices. Put him in charge of your harvest. Let him draw up the contract with the cutter. Let him handle the sale with the mill. You'll almost certainly get a better harvesting job, and a bigger check, this way than if you go it alone the first time.

When you—or the forester, who is your agent—are ready to contract with a logger who will come onto your land and harvest trees, be sure the contract is a properly written and executed document. This is to protect you and your woods as well as the logger you hire. Logging contracts—often called Timber Sale Agreements—vary greatly according to the circumstances of different parties to them. Nevertheless, here are some items that should be treated in a complete, well-drawn agreement: the logger is to cut marked trees only; he is to cut stumps so as to leave your or the forester's marks (in spray paint, usually) on the stumps, proving that the cut trees were marked for harvest; the logger's access roads and the landings where he assembles logs for shipment are to be approved by you or your forester; unused tree tops and branches ("slash") are to be lopped close to the ground (no higher than four feet, say); the logger is to furnish a copy of the mill's count of delivered logs from your job; he is to repair any damage he does to existing roads, fences, and the like, and he is to do so within a specified time after the harvest is finished; you are not liable for damages resulting from any injury to the logger or his employees suffered on your property or elsewhere in connection with your harvest (get a copy of the logger's workmen's compensation insurance policy).

ACCESS

Working in hardwoods or softwoods to prune or thin, you have probably been content to enter the woods wherever it was convenient. If you're thinking of a timber harvest, however, it is time to think of access to the woodlot for vehicles. You'll probably have to make some roads. It must be obvious in looking at any piece of woodland that no one is going to use equipment in it if there is no easy access. It is also plain that getting logs out without a road of some kind is next to impossible.

Some like to have everything done all at once and nothing first —boom, finished. I like to move along step by step, always having some important improvement ahead. In trying to complete the perfect whole, instantly, it is necessary to have lots of money and lots of help, and to be omniscient. It is necessary to foresee all problems and to take steps to remedy them. I think that no one is that smart, not even the professional forester with many successful jobs under his belt. I think that the instant woodlot is both impossible and unwise. I have said, again and again, that forest land is complex. I do not feel that you can or should create an instant diamond in the form of a finished and perfect woodlot. These considerations are especially pertinent in discussing road-making, for in no other woodland occupation does haste make more waste, more quickly.

In making roads in the woods, I spend a lot of time planning and looking over the lay of the land before I break out the chainsaw and call the bulldozer operator. It's best to begin by laying out your road system on a map. Take it easy, think small, and take short steps. I certainly do not want you to hire the bulldozer and just move in, making roads more or less at random. Such an action would be expensive and too many mistakes would be made. A lot of damage could be done to trees, soil, and watercourses.

You need a model for the road system you're planning. Thinking small, look at a sugar maple leaf. Notice how the veins run. The network reaches every part of the leaf. In general, this is what your roads and trails should do. Cut out the leaf material leaving the skeleton of the main veins. Use them as a template and lay them on your map. There will be difficulty with the scale, of course. What I am trying to suggest is that your road network— roads, skid trails, and paths—should reach every part of your woodlot, eventually anyway. Naturally, the arrangement of veins will not exactly suit the lay of the land. I am merely trying to get you to visualize the road system before you do anything on the

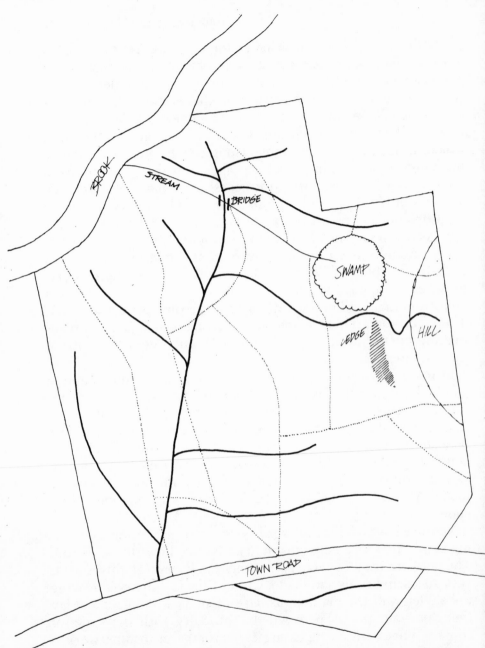

Layout of road system in the hypothetical woodlot shown in the map in Chapter IV. The roads are planned to extend to all areas of the woodlot, ascending the ledgy hill at right by zig-zags to minimize the slope.

ground. Many survey maps do not indicate wet spots, ledges, or contours. There may be special plants that you wish to save, too.

Having fooled around mentally, go to the woods. Proceed to the point where you plan to enter your woodlot. This can be a public road, an old log road, or some natural forest opening. Look, please, look. Deer trails can give you a lot of help. Deer have a most astute way of making a graded climb, avoiding wet spots and ledge. Who wants to get mud on those shiny black hoofs or crack them on sharp stone? The deer may give you your first clue as to the path of easiest access to all corners of your woodlot.

Maybe some far off soul made a real woods road. So much the better, although they are hard to find in the summer. But when the leaves are off or when there is a slight dusting of snow, man-made traces leap to the discerning eye. Usually old roads are pretty sensible: the old-timers did not want to wear out the yoke of oxen or the team, so they tried to avoid steep grades and water-courses. Go thou and do likewise, bearing the arrangement of the leaf veins in mind.

The game trail or the old woods road could well be the main drag of your system. For the nonce, forget about parallel roads, feeders, or loops.

Get some old rags. An old bed sheet is fine. Make two-inch-wide strips, each maybe two feet long. Put these in a basket, bag, or your pocket. In the woods, tie the first cloth strip at about eye level at the point of entry. Move along your chosen route, but, before you lose sight of the first strip, tie another and so proceed.

Roads in the woodlot. The best roads curve gently, avoid sharp corners, and allow room to maneuver at turns.

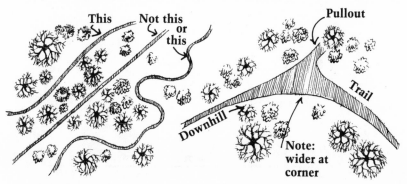

As you amble along, you may find ledge or a glacial erratic (large boulder left at random by a glacier). Make a wide and gentle meander around it—no sharp turns, please. Life is more complicated if you come across a spring, seep, or brook. Veer around such, if possible. If necessary, re-route. If it is a brook, you will have to make a culvert. I will come to construction and related matters in a bit. As of this moment you are only laying out a trail so no construction is necessary.

If you arrive at an unavoidable steep grade, zig-zag, making the turns wide. A good way to judge this is to pretend that you are

It's best to clear woods roads of brush and overhanging branches to greater heights than may seem necessary, to allow for snowfall's raising the level of the road and to accommodate different users: vehicles, riders, skiers, and others.

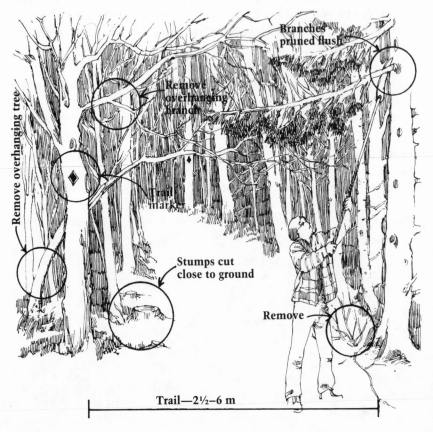

Trail—2½–6 m

going to make a step turn on skis. Give yourself plenty of room for the turn. Naturally, you are remembering to tie the cloth strips to mark the route as you move along.

At last you have arrived at the outer edge of your property or have gone about as far as you wish to in this general direction. Turn around.

On the return trip, make any corrections you wish by relocating the cloth strips, widening a turn, perhaps. While retracing your steps, you might as well do some small bit of work. With your ever-present hand clippers, nip off any branches which swat you in the face, but resist the temptation to do any heavy clearing. The terrain may look different on subsequent trips.

Another day and you are back on the job bearing clippers, axe, and Meylan saw. Pretend you are on horseback. Cut brush, overhead or side branches which would bother you if you really were on horseback. If such impediments are out of the way for a horseback rider, they are out of the way for the ski tourer, too. Presto: riding, hiking, ski touring trail.

Let the matter sit for a while. Scout around some to make sure your main maple vein is on the best possible site. When you are convinced, bring in the heavier battalions—chainsaw and axe. If it is absolutely necessary to cut sizable trees which would impede the roadway, cut them off about three feet from the ground and salvage the wood for fuel. The high stump will give the bulldozer that will finish the road some leverage to aid in removal.

The original trail is now eight to ten feet wide, free of brush and branches, and will be free of stumps when the bulldozer clears them off and smooths the ground. When frozen, logs can safely be skidded over it. If money is no object, a good, permanent road should be graveled. Sometimes, with light and infrequent use, planting grass seed will be sufficient to protect against erosion. The decision will rest on local conditions, use, and pocketbook.

CONSTRUCTION: WATER BARS

If you're making roads in the woodlot you'll need to protect them against erosion by constructing water bars and culverts, and by ditching and contouring the road. You also may need to build simple bridges.

A water bar is a shallow ditch lying diagonally across the road. The higher end is on the uphill side of the road. The upper edge of the ditch has a very gradual grade so that water can flow into the trench or ditch. The lower edge is also gradual, but is built up a bit with the material taken from the ditch. This permits occasional surface waters to be guided off the road which helps to control erosion below. The contour of a water bar is that of an extremely shallow U: for a water bar six inches across the bottom the top might be two feet across. The depth will vary with each site.

I do not mean to try to tell my grandmother how to suck eggs, but many people who buy forest land have not had the opportunity to see and understand what takes place in a heavy rain or with a rapid snow melt. What you are trying to do is to prevent water from standing on or running down the road. This is in response to the dictum of the engineer—get water off and away from any road. I am not always so agreeable to the engineering point of view, but I accept this principle as true gospel.

In addition to having water bars, a good road is not really flat.

A water bar in cross section and from above. The built-up lip on the downhill side holds water that the slant of the water bar directs off the road.

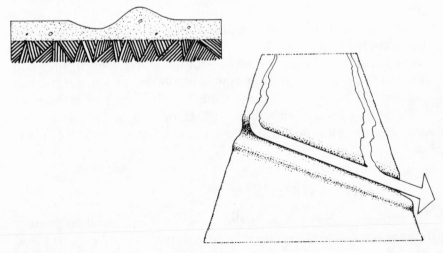

It is mildly rounded so that it will shed rain. At some locations it is a good idea to ditch the sides of a road to promote quicker drainage. A good bulldozer operator knows how to do this without tearing up the entire county and without damaging nearby trees. A poor operator, overcome with a massive power complex induced by his powerful machine, will do more harm than good. For short distances, be labor intensive. A shovel does a fine job at ditching and is cheap. Besides, it builds the biceps.

Now the new road is crowned slightly, ditched, and provided with water bars. In some spots—where there is permanent running water or a gully—a culvert is called for. In extreme cases, a bridge may be necessary.

CONSTRUCTION: CULVERTS

I do not know if this is still possible, but years ago I used to ask the road commissioner of the town to give or sell me culverts which were no longer adequate for a heavily traveled public road. The discarded culvert might be rusty or pitted, but it may still be satisfactory in a new site that is a little-traveled private road. When the secondhand culvert is installed, place the pitted, rusty side uphill. The downhill side and bottom should be sound, and this is usually the way culverts start to deteriorate—bottom first.

To install the culvert, dig by machine or by hand a trench about twice as wide as the culvert and as deep as needed for the site. Again, place the culvert gently on the diagonal, with a slight downhill slope. Put stones, rocks or stony gravel on both sides, firmly. Top the works with good gravel. It does no harm to mound this a bit. It will pack. Anyway, this is not a speedway.

If there is no used culvert available, you might buy a new one, but I hope your purse is full. I settle for making culverts from local materials and a bit of labor. To make a log culvert, cut two straight logs as long as needed to carry across the road with a couple of feet overlap at each end. Dig the ditch, but wider than before. Place the logs—I use hemlock about ten inches in diameter—parallel in the ditch and a foot or so apart. Place flat rocks over the logs. Cover with gravel, mounded as usual.

You can also make a culvert of stone, building two small parallel retaining walls to be covered with flat rocks or a heavy plank. Cover with mounded gravel. Or, make a box of heavy planks, install, cover, and mound.

Any of these culverts will last quite a long time. Some that I installed in 1950 are still serviceable. You can help them survive by putting stones at the outfall and by lining the entry point with stones to guide the water and to prevent erosion.

CONSTRUCTION: BRIDGES

A culvert is really a little bridge. Making one will give you a clue as to how to make a real bridge for a more sizable stream. Bridge-building can be as big a job as you want to make it. For my part, I aim to be a good forester, not a civil engineer. I have made simple bridges as follows: make a graded trench along the streambed wide enough for the expected maximum flow of water; throw logs across the trench, spaced as tightly together as possible and making a span twice as wide as any vehicle you might use; lay at least four feet of bridge-log on either bank; cover the

A simple log bridge. Large logs are chinked with saplings and the whole is covered with earth.

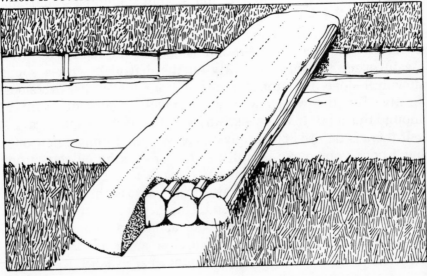

logs with a few feet of earth. To keep the dirt from falling through the logs, the logs should be laid with the small ends alternating; fit saplings into any cracks. The logs should be straight and should have as little taper as possible. They should be at least six to eight inches thick. I've used poplar logs, but any handy logs will do. The dirt is what holds this bridge together, really: no spikes are needed. This bridge will rot, sure, but mine have been good for ten years. Material and time costs are small, and the bridge is easily replaced. For any bridge, fill the ends of the span with earth and gravel so the approaches to the bridge are gradual. You don't want to bump down onto the bridge with a heavy vehicle.

Log bridges like the one I've described are temporary structures. Made well, with treated logs or with logs that are naturally slow to rot, such a bridge will be good for ten years or more. It's important, though, to keep a careful eye on bridges like these, examining them for rot, and checking banks often—especially in the spring—to make sure they're still strong.

Now, alas, you have come to a stiff grade and, according to advice, the road zigs and zags, but it still retains its downhill slope, modified but still there. If nothing is done, vehicles and logs will slide off the road on the downhill side. All in all, there will be problems and damaged trees on the lower side.

To correct such a situation, have the bulldozer slice away a segment on the uphill side and push the material across to the downhill side. This makes a relatively flat surface—rounded, really—lightly ditched on the uphill side. Again, for short distances, a pick and shovel job is both adequate and cheap.

As of this labored moment, we have widened the main road, rounded its surface, spread some gravel, and have constructed water bars, culverts, and bridges as required. If you have been careful you have a heavy-duty road on which you can safely travel with a team, tractor, or light truck. Possibly, if you have been extra careful, you might trust it to take care of a logging truck. In a way, this is a bright idea, because logging trucks carry loading equipment and can load up right in the woods. Despite this convenience, however, I do not care for logging trucks in small woodlots. Logging trucks are great lumbering things, somewhat less than stable. They can do a lot of damage to themselves, their

Filling and leveling the trail

Side-hill roads. The drawings show different ways of leveling a road that crosses a slope.

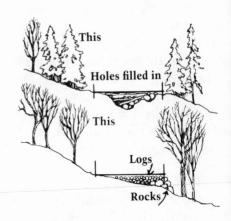

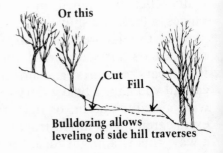

Bulldozing allows leveling of side hill traverses

operators, and to the terrain. Let's decide, here and now, to relegate logging trucks to the public road.

SKID TRAILS

Once your main woods road is finished, you'll need to plan for skid trails: temporary lanes along which logs will be dragged from the stump to the location where they're loaded up for shipping out of the woods. Skid trails, like the main drag, should avoid ledges, wet spots, and sharp turns. Even on a carefully planned and constructed trail logs will fishtail from side to side as they're winched along. They can bang into trail-side trees, damaging them. To combat this, inferior logs can be placed as bumpers against trees along the skid trail.

Bulldozers and log skidders—even in the hands of careful operators—play hell with the forest soil, gouging ruts that invite erosion. Carefully made woods roads and trails help minimize the damage. In snow country, logging in winter also helps. Frozen earth is hard, and the snow protects the earth beneath it from the equipment. Even on frozen ground, however, bulldozers and skidders will produce gullies which can grow if not cared for after the machines depart. You'll need to take a shovel and rake to these ruts.

Building roads and putting in culverts and such is hard work. To make it go more easily you can approach the task in one of two ways. You can hire the owner of the biggest, mightiest bulldozer in town and turn him loose in your woodlot (I hope you're ready to write a big check when he's done, and I hope he's left you with a few trees fit to harvest). You can also slow down, ponder where you're going, and do the work in small, careful bits rather than in one headlong rush. By now I don't have to tell you which alternative has my own favor.

VII | 𝟂𝟂

Enjoying Woodlots

IN ADDITION TO, and along with, managing your woods to produce usable and salable products you can increase their usefulness for recreation by any number of steps. I have experimented with several kinds of recreational woodlot management (to give it a fancy name), and I know whereof I speak.

Perhaps our most novel adventure in woodlot management has been turning sections of our woodlot into a kind of do-it-yourself arboretum or tree-collection. I have always admired the diversity and adaptation of native trees and shrubs. They can be both useful and decorative. Because they're natives, they are also relatively trouble-free. They do not have to be coddled.

Since the natives demand no quarter, I decided to make a collection of native trees and shrubs, to provide forage and shelter for birds, to protect plant species and communities threatened by development, and to create a pleasant setting. I am not exceedingly strict or discriminating about the species I've selected for inclusion; even the experts are puzzled about what species are native and what have been introduced and adapted so well that home-country identification is difficult.

I set up a seedbed and nursery on our six-acre plot in Woodstock, Vermont. I started seeds of native trees, shrubs, and smaller plants in the seedbed. I found I had to give some care to seedbed construction. Mice love seeds, so do chipmunks, so the seedbed must have a rodent-proof top and bottom, of wire screening. I made a small separate box for each different type of seed, because some seeds germinate quickly and some lurk in the ground for a year or more. I marked which seeds were in which boxes, and I kept the beds weeded and shaded (too much sun can dry out and kill seedlings). I moved the most vigorous of my seedlings to the nursery after they'd got a good start, and transplanted them out to various locations around our property when I judged they could stand competition from other plants and the unfriendly attentions of mice, porcupines, and deer. Each shrub or tree is put into a suitable site; some prefer wet soil, some dry; some need direct sun, some shade.

I now have some fifty kinds of native trees, shrubs, and smaller plants growing along our woodland walk, including five kinds of maple, various viburnums, dogwoods, cherries, birches, as well as butternut, ash, beech, thorn apple, ferns, trilliums, jack-in-the-pulpit, and Canada lilies. Since my aim is to increase the local supply of trees or plants and not simply rearrange it, I have raised most of my specimens from wild seed or cuttings, with an occasional purchase from a nursery. Transplanting wild plants seldom works. It's a good way to get in trouble with your neighbors, for one thing. For another, it's hard work: stones and roots get in the way, and it is nigh onto impossible in digging a wild sapling to remove a satisfactory ball of earth with the intact root system. If you must try to move a wild tree or shrub, be sure to get permission from whoever owns the land it's on. Do the transplanting in the spring, dig up the root system with care, and plant it with care, trying to fill all air pockets around the roots with soil. Prune the transplant's branches to make up for roots that it has lost in the move. And be prepared for failure: transplanting from the wild is too often a laborious way of killing whatever it is you've tried to transplant. There are easier ways of killing trees.

It seems to me to be worthwhile in making a collection of native trees and shrubs to fill in with the smaller companion plants. This is why I have a fine fern collection and small stands

A section of the author's arboretum of native trees and other plants at Woodstock, Vermont.

of foam flower, trillium, jack-in-the-pulpit, and Canada lilies. Columbine does well. I have no luck with marsh marigold, but the bottle gentian does well, and so does meadow rue if I can protect it from the deer.

Arboretum-building is a very satisfying occupation. I pore over the plant lists from various nurseries and seed collectors during the winter. I plan what to buy and where I will put the purchases. I usually plant seed when it is ripe and the purchased plants when they are available. My efforts from my own little nursery are planted out in the spring. All this activity is well within the scope of one who has lately become an octogenarian.

IMPROVING WILDLIFE HABITAT

There are other ways to improve your woodlot as a place of recreation besides arboretum-building. Most of them involve improving the woodlot as habitat—for wild birds, animals, and fish, and for people. Improvement of wildlife habitat in a woodlot is quite consistent with a judicious program of intensive woodlot forestry. Generally, it consists of providing shelter, food, and water in a relatively undisturbed setting.

Consider the fish. If you have running water in your woods, you may have trout habitat. If you own or adopt a brook, you can often improve its ability to carry brook trout, rainbows, and brown trout. Even a small brook may do. Quite often, in the northeast, it is not even necessary to stock a brook. Improve the habitat for trout, and they will do the rest. Doing so is fun and easy. If there are small boys of any age in your family, they will fall for this activity.

Some day, when the water is clear and the light good, put on waders and walk slowly and thoughtfully in the bed of the brook. You are looking for relatively deep holes or pools. If none exist, or if they are few, look for places where these might be created. You should also seek out small natural falls or riffles, undercut banks, and brush overhang.

List these features on a sketch map of the brook. For such purposes, a few hundred yards of brook will do, but a whole mile is better.

Small brush alongside a trout brook is beneficial. The brush protects the bank from erosion, shades the water, and often harbors bugs, which fall into the water to become trout provender. If no brush exists, consider planting native dogwoods, viburnums, and willows. Take note that big trees and small brooks are not compatible. The trees use too much water, and freshets tend to undermine their roots. This may cause the trees to fall into the brook, damaging the bank in the process. While shade is beneficial, it can be supplied by brush, so large brookside trees are candidates for the woodpile when time and energy permit.

Patches of sunlight on a brook are beneficial. Openings in the brush for sunlight should be relatively small, and there is no reason why they cannot coincide with a place to cast, arranged either for up- or downstream fishing. Cut the brush and mow the grass and weeds from time to time in a small area giving access to one of your favorite pools. If artfully done, this will look natural and will immensely facilitate fishing. In cutting, do not forget to allow for the backward sweep of your line.

Varied and supportive living conditions almost guarantee a wildlife population. Nevertheless, to enhance trout habitat, it is necessary to think like a trout. If you were a trout in a small brook on a hot day, where would you go? Attractive spots would be a spring hole or seep where the water is cold, or under an overhanging bank. Another possibility would be near a large boulder. If your stream lacks these amenities, you can provide them. Most brooks have small springs and seeps in their beds. Seek them out. A clue to their presence may be a cluster of fish seeking cooler water, or bubble action in rock, sand, or mud. You can enhance their value by a little delicate digging or prying with a crowbar. If there are no large boulders, insert some into the streambed, preferably in the middle of the stream. The water will speed up and flow around the boulder, creating a little eddy where a trout can take a siesta. Food floating in the stream will also tend to concentrate in such an eddy, giving the trout more leisure time in which to grow fat. You may find a clay bank that's only slightly undercut. By forcing water against such a bank, one can get the stream to do the necessary excavation work.

A wing dam of logs or rocks will divert the water so that a nice hiding place results. Wing or V dams can be placed in tandem if stream conditions permit. Another useful device is a straight dam across the brook. The function of the straight dam is not to cause water to back up above the dam, but to give water something to flow over. As water crosses the straight dam, it comes in contact with air and picks up oxygen. Quite often the limiting factor to trout development is not water temperature, but lack of oxygen in the water. The straight dam increases the oxygen supply, making it possible for trout to survive even in fairly high temperatures.

Another reason for building various structures in the stream is to change the course of the water and to increase its speed. Even the casual stream-watcher will notice that when water spreads out, it slows down. More area is exposed to sun and air, resulting in two undesirable conditions for trout: the water becomes warmer and, with the reduced speed, the capacity of the water to

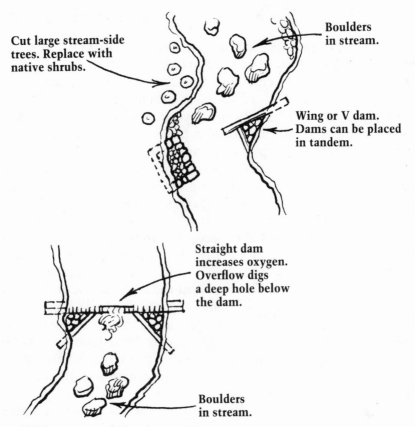

Cut large stream-side trees. Replace with native shrubs.

Boulders in stream.

Wing or V dam. Dams can be placed in tandem.

Straight dam increases oxygen. Overflow digs a deep hole below the dam.

Boulders in stream.

Boulders and simple dams in trout water. Both create turbulence and speed stream flow, which improve the stream as trout habitat by adding oxygen to the water and providing hiding places.

carry soil along is lessened. Siltation results, and this is a great hazard for trout because the silt covers potential spawning areas and smothers insect larvae, which are prime trout food. In improving trout habitat it is important to keep the water moving along smartly, but not so fast that trout eggs and trout food are washed away. Narrowing the channel also tends to concentrate food supplies, making them more readily available for the fish.

After food and shelter, proper spawning beds are the next requirement for trout management. Trout need gravel and sand, well washed and well aerated, for spawning. If your stream lacks sand and gravel, you can buy a truckload of washed river gravel. If it is clean and sharp, it need not be sorted as to size. Find a pool with a fairly rapid flow and spread the gravel evenly over the bottom of this pool. When stream action has given the gravel a natural look, trout will probably oblige by using it as a spawning bed. To ensure the safety of the unhatched eggs and the well-being of the trout fry, the bed—in addition to a sandy bottom—must also have well-oxygenated, moving water. It should contain cool water and be free from heavy silting.

It would not be fair to the reader to run off without saying how wing and straight dams are made, although there is no single design that is always satisfactory. Much depends on your inventiveness and the requirements of your particular brook.

To help make manmade structures acceptable to fish, they should look as natural as possible. This means that native materials, such as logs and boulders, should be used. Usually, these are readily available on the site.

Let's start with a V dam of rock. The upstream leg of the V should incline slightly downstream. The downstream leg can take any convenient angle. The point of the V should be not more than halfway across the stream. If the bank of the stream is composed of earth, make an excavation for each leg about two feet into the stream bank. Using local stone, make a rough wall just a little higher than the prevailing water level. Fill the space between the legs of the V with rock to add strength to the structure. If the stream bank permits, you can put two of these dams in tandem, one on each bank. This will cause the water to zig-zag, giving it more speed and also creating eddies.

A similar dam can be made with logs. The ends are dug into the bank. The ends in the stream are notched, log-cabin fashion, and the horizontal spaces between the logs are filled with flat stones. The space between the two log legs is also filled with stones. It helps to drill a hole in each log near the tip in the stream and to line these holes up so that a reinforcing rod may be driven down through the holes to further anchor the logs against the power of the stream. V dams must be as sturdy as you can make them.

The straight dam is somewhat easier to build. Again, it is useful to dig into the stream bank on each side to anchor the dam.

Lay stones or logs across the stream and bring the level to that of the prevailing water flow or a little higher. If the dam is of logs, chink in with small stones and strengthen it with stones on the upstream side. Not only will the water flowing over the dam pick up more oxygen, which is then released into the stream below the dam, but if the brook bed permits, this falling water will also dig a hole—ideal for trout. These holes bubble with oxygen, concentrate trout food, and help to protect fish from all but the most determined predator.

All these actions—encouraging brush, cutting large trees, providing shelter and spawning beds, increasing the food and oxygen supply—should enable trout to prosper as never before. If you are in doubt about whether your efforts have increased the trout population in your brook, perhaps you can inveigle the Fish and Game people to test the stream by electric shock. The test is conducted on a single pool. Any fish in the pool appear belly-up, stunned but unhurt. With as little handling as possible, the fish are weighed and sexed. In this way you can obtain a base count to refer to after your habitat improvements have been in place for several years. You will be amazed and pleased at the improvement. If there are no fish in your stream, stock the stream, but only after your improvements have had a chance to mellow a bit.

There are a couple of small sidelights. Each pool tends to have a dominant fish that pre-empts the best feeding spot and the best place to hide. If the dominant fish is caught, another immediately takes its place. If you observe closely you can actually see this take place. If the trout in your stream seem to be getting smaller after you have set up your stream improvements, you have been too successful. Too many trout survive. The answer to this is to fish more heavily and remove the excess population. As you do so, the survivors will become more wary and more choosy, and you will discover that a good habitat tends to favor the survival of the better and brighter fish.

Upland birds, like trout, are wildlife that thrive in a fairly specialized habitat, one that a woodlot owner may help to provide if he has the essentials. For game birds like grouse, as for any other wildlife, the essentials are water, food, shelter, in that order. Grouse prefer a variety of terrain to range over, from swampy wetland, to open fields, to softwoods, to hardwoods. A ruffed grouse may require as much as forty acres of range. You may not have a spread that size to devote to grouse, but you can make your portion of a potential grouse range more hospitable by encouraging the kinds of environment that grouse need at different seasons.

You want to provide hardwoods, softwoods, meadow, marsh, and orchard, all with a varied exposure to the sun. In much of New England one can find a suitable meadow. It may be difficult to keep that meadow from rushing back to forest, but it is essential to do so, because even a small meadow, preferably with a gentle tilt to the south, is essential in grouse habitat. To keep the meadow open, mow it every three years or so. One need not be nasty neat about this process so long as the clearing is kept in the early stages of plant succession. Grouse use a meadow as a source of weed seeds, insects, and small fruits, so if there is a tendency for wild strawberries, elderberries, blackcaps, blackberries, and raspberries to appear, do not discourage them, for such is the grouse concept of heaven. Do beware, however. The minute invaders such as white pine, gray birch, wild cherry, red cedar, or poplar put in an appearance—mow. These plants have a place and a function for grouse purposes but not in a grouse meadow.

At the edge of the meadow, encourage berry plants and add, if you will, wild grapes and other vines producing edible seeds. On behalf of the grouse population, you are after a wild tangle between the open and the woods. In the second rank of the plant profile encourage shrubs and small trees such as the various viburnums and dogwoods, the hop hornbeam and staghorn sumac and the thorn apples. In the rear rank you want the true forest trees.

In season, the open field provides food and sites for sunning and dusting. The line of small fruits and shrubs provides nesting places and a safe nursery. Soon after hatching, the chicks and the hen leave the rather rude nest; the chicks grow fast on the varied diet—which is essential for health—and the tangle provides security. A grouse chick can make its way through tiny openings in the tangle of vines, canes, and shrubs, which inhibits or stops the most determined feral cat or hungry fox.

It is no trick to establish the necessary plants if they do not now grow between meadow and forest. In time, natural succession will do the trick. If you are in a hurry and have lots of money and not much muscle, buy the plants and have them planted. Otherwise, prepare yourself for a high failure rate, dig wild plants, and move them yourself.

Man likes to put things in straight rows, but this is not nature's way; it is better to plant in irregular clumps. An irregular line is more pleasing to the eye, and when the plants grow and merge, the curving edges form protective coves, which look more natural.

What trees and plants should you try to establish for grouse? In our section of the country, hop hornbeam is the year-round favorite. Grouse eat the buds in winter, the flowers in spring, and the fruit in the summer and fall. In other areas, poplar is said to be a favorite.

The softwoods are mainly for shelter from weather extremes and cover from aerial predators. The hardwoods provide buds for winter food and insects for the summer diet. With one or two exceptions, the hardwoods and the softwoods do not mix well, since their growing requirements are different.

Shelter from weather and enemies must also be near a winter food supply, which consists almost entirely of hardwood tree buds. Our local grouse prefer the buds of ash and maple. Of course, persistent vine and shrub seeds are also eaten. These include juniper berries, highbush cranberry drupes, frozen grapes, and staghorn sumac berries. Among small fruits and trees, dogwood, viburnums, alders, thorn apple, serviceberry, elderberry, blackberry, and raspberry are also desirable. An abandoned apple orchard is a grouse paradise. Wild apple trees are even better, because they tend to hold their fruit longer than tended trees. Grouse eat apple seeds and the insects that frequent apple trees, so if you have an old orchard, keep it from going back to forest by removing the invading species. If you have time and energy, you might mulch and fertilize a few trees. A little pruning of dead wood will also enhance the yield. Who knows? You might like some of the old-time apples as much as the deer and the grouse do.

It was customary to plant orchards on a south-facing slope to get as much light as possible and to permit cold air to flow downhill away from the orchard. Anybody who has an old orchard could take advantage of these factors to create an abutting wild-life island. This island could be the connecting link between various elements of grouse habitat. It might connect the shelterbelt of softwoods with the meadow, or the hardwood forest with the meadow or marsh. In my definition, a wildlife island is a sunny spot in the late spring, protected from the wind, and planted with the various food plants mentioned above. (I was all too successful in the creation of such a place many years ago. An inspection of animal tracks in the late winter showed that every native animal had visited the island, and the deer ate all the food plants.)

I have mentioned that some form of wetland is a necessity because its role is varied and important, so if you do not have one, it is a good idea to create a bit of swamp. The wetland's first contribution is a varied flora, which produces a varied fauna. The wetland provides a degree of cover and a lot of varied food. The ideal location for a swamp would be below the orchard and connected with it by a travel lane of food and cover plants. Seepage from a spring or diverted water from a brook can be used to make a small swamp. To do so, make a small mound of earth downhill from a spring or brook. Let the water enter the resulting depression. Plant it or not as you choose; given time, nature will take care of the matter by planting rushes, sedges, and other wetland plants. Open water is not necessary. A nice soggy wet spot is necessary as a site for airborne seeds. Incidentally, woodcock will also appreciate the spot.

If you do create a better grouse habitat where there are already some grouse, this population will automatically increase to fill the new niche. It does not necessarily mean a boom-or-bust grouse population. In my experience, in an ideal habitat the grouse population is almost stable. The population will increase to utilize the increase in food and cover. Natural predation will also increase and will prevent disease by eliminating the sick. Natural predation will also improve the bloodlines by removing the dim-witted, so do not be hard on the natural predators. They, too, must live and they, too, have a proper function in grouse ecology.

You will have to do something about feral cats. Because farming is on the decline, house and barn cats can no longer subsist on the rodents that populate working farms, and they turn feral.

They do more harm to game and song birds than any other single predator. Cats, like man, hunt for pleasure and must be controlled.

Another reason that a relatively constant level in the grouse population is possible in an ideal habitat is the grouse dispersal system. Annually, a grouse family group breaks up. Something suddenly triggers an impulse in young grouse to get away from home and mother, and as a consequence the young birds take off, more or less in a straight line of flight (they sometimes hit buildings and other obstacles). What makes them stop, I know not. Maybe they see a nice spot to live in. Maybe they just get tired. Anyway, they are away from the old terrain and in a new one, and this is a factor in the maintenance of a stable population.

As with improving trout habitat, the important point is to create ideal living conditions and then let the birds do the rest.

I have discussed improving woodlots as trout and grouse habitat at some length because I have experience in both these subjects, not because they are in any way preferred for woodlot owners. Improving grouse habitat, indeed, will also improve conditions for any number of wild things, including turkeys, quail, rabbits, squirrels, and deer, and the predators of all of these. In the woods, when you make one thing better you often make other things better, too; it's the flip side of the far-reaching and largely unknowable damage that can be done to forest land by careless, fast-buck management—about which I've unburdened myself sufficiently in earlier chapters.

TRAILS AND CAMPSITES

Practically any recreational use of woodland will entail laying out trails. Woodlots are compatible with all kinds: hiking, horseback riding, skiing, and snowshoeing.

One of the principal reasons for making a trail is to grant access to the land without doing it any harm. If the trail is well laid out and obvious to any potential user, the trail will be followed, and random soil compaction, the trampling of rare plants, and the damage to young stock are avoided or, at least, controlled.

Up to a point, woodland trails may improve wildlife habitat. Trails can increase the edge area in which low-growing plants will grow in the sunlight admitted by the trail opening, providing food and shelter. In a dry, sunny spot on a trail a sun bath may attract many birds including grouse. Humans are not the only creatures that use a trail. Almost every wild creature I know will use a grassy woodland trail for much the same reason we do: it is easier to get around.

Making trails is an art in itself. For trail planning, refer to the advice on road building in the preceding chapter: avoid sharp turns; take advantage of existing game trails; lay the route out with flags before you start clearing brush and trees so you can reconsider. The idea behind woods *roads* is to provide access by vehicle to all parts of the woodlot, while the idea behind laying out a woodland trail is to go wherever fancy leads. Still, some of the rules of road building should be borne in mind in planning trails. Especially important is to avoid placing your trail so that it promotes erosion: keep turns gradual, therefore, go upslope gradually, and avoid wet places if you can.

You shouldn't have to cut a lot of trees to make a trail; after all, in a manner of speaking you're making the trail so you can get a better look at those trees. You will be chopping brush, though, and pruning low branches. If you cut trailside branches high enough so that they will not bother a horseman (say 12 to 16 feet), you will also satisfy the ski tourer when several feet of snow have raised the trail level. Any trail which satisfies both the rider and the ski tourer will do nicely for birding, botanizing, and other nature study. It will also suit the snowshoer.

You can improve one or more campsites in your woods, selecting likely spots to which you'll repair when you're in need of a mild overnight outdoor adventure, and which you can gussy up as much or as little as you please. Though your woodlot campsite is apt to be permanent or semipermanent, in picking a spot you should keep in mind the features of the best temporary campsites. Most important, choose level, dry ground. Nothing is worse than sleeping on an incline, unless it's sleeping on damp ground (*trying* to sleep, I should say). Avoid grassy spots, for they're damp. Look for a well-drained, level spot. In the fall dry leaves make good ground cover for a campsite if they're kept clear of

At the Hawk's Hill Demonstration Woodlot, the author skis across a stream on a simple footbridge.

any fire. Pick a spot that's sheltered from high winds, but don't camp in still air—at least not in the warm months—or you'll be prey to bugs. Try for a spot where the air is moving: breezy, but not windy. Water and dead wood for fuel nearby are a help. Stay away from big trees that can draw lightning and whose heavy branches can drop at inconvenient moments, and stay away from rock overhangs that can shed boulders.

To fix up a campsite for repeated use, you can simply kick the biggest stones away from where you're going to sleep and call it done, you can erect a fancy cabin or wheel in your Winnebago, and you can do everything in between. I like a certain degree of comfort, and for me and those of my tastes simple pole lean-tos and plank platforms for tents are easy to make and afford the luxury we crave. I've even built permanent, open-front log shel- ters for camping in the woods. They take some doing, but they make for a pleasant camp. They also gave me a use for small pine thinned from one of our young stands, thereby upholding a fun- damental tenet of intensive woodlot forestry: a use for every tree that grows in the woods.

If you go in for shelter building you may be guided by my experience. I picked an arbitrary size for my first shelter—12 feet wide and 15 feet deep. The height of the open side was 8 feet, and at the back the height was 5 feet. This established the slant of the roof. The materials were stone for the base and—with clay as a binder—for the chimney; logs for the sides; rough boards for the roof deck; building paper; and shakes. The fasteners were roofing nails and large spikes, long enough to fasten two layers of logs together.

I began by collecting rocks for the base and chimney. I found a nearby stone wall I could cannibalize, so I decided to make the base walls 3 feet high and about 18 inches wide, capped with flat stones to make a fairly even base for the logs.

With the stone base in place it was time to make the next move, which was to mark and cut the logs. The logs came from thinnings in a red pine plantation that Elizabeth and I planted in 1947. The shelter was built in 1961 or 1962. The logs could be made 16 feet long and at least 4 inches at the top end. It was difficult to guess how many such logs would be needed for a

An open-faced camp shelter (this one without a chimney) built by the author at Amity Pond, Pomfret, Vermont.

shelter, so I cut forty trees. Surplus, I figured, could be used to make benches or a rough table for the shelter.

The logs were trucked to a nearby mill and a thin slab was taken off two opposite sides. Some logs were cut through and through to make inch-thick boards for the roof deck. If the bark had not come off in this process, it was removed. The slabbed logs were 4 inches thick, but some were wider than others, so I had to sort out eighteen of the wider logs. Six logs on three sides made the side walls and back 2 feet high in logs, and I had a 3-foot high stone base, so six courses of logs gave me a back wall 5 feet high.

Starting on either side wall, I placed one log on the stone base so that the front end was flush with the stone. I chinked this log with small stones so that it was firmly seated on the stone base. Then I butted the next log to the first along the back wall and chinked it. The third log I placed on the remaining side wall, and chinked also. I didn't worry about the overhanging log ends at this point. They served as a sort of ladder for other work and could be cut flush later. I took pains to get the first three logs level, firm, and ready for the next tier of logs. The second and subsequent tiers were spiked to the first. The shelter had no frame of vertical members. I started the second tier on the opposite side from that on which the first tier was laid. This made an overlap at each corner, which helped to make the shelter tight.

When the three walls reached 5 feet in height, I nailed a board on each side of the shelter's opening, extending 8 feet high from the ground. Then I nailed another board from the top of the vertical eight-footer to the back wall. This marked the angle for the roof. Each log on both sides now had to be measured and cut on a slant to meet the roof angle. I spiked each log in place and continued until the peak was reached. Now there was a firm base for the roof rafters, and the marking boards could be removed.

I was not fussy about the spacing of the roof rafters. They do have to support a lot of snow, and small boys like to clamber onto the roof, so setting them on 2-foot centers seemed all right. The rafters hung over on each side. When the overhang was roofed over it helped protect the sides of the shelter from rain. The roof rafters were spiked to the walls, helping to ensure that the walls were plumb.

With all the rafters in place, I nailed on the boards to form the roof deck. Since the logs were cut through and through to make these boards, the boards weren't square, and they had to be alternated small end to big end to cover the roof. With the roof deck finished, I put on roofing paper, then shakes, which were nailed on leaving 6 inches to weather.

It was not necessary to have a chimney. An outside fireplace would have been much less work. I liked the idea of a chimney made the old, pioneer-style way, however. I used clay from a pond I had made. In the process of digging the pond I had found some good clay. This, puddled with water from the pond, served instead of cement mortar.

I placed the chimney just outside the open front of the shelter, and to one side. In making the chimney base, I laid up the stones so that the base was bigger than the chimney. About a foot from ground level I made a level area with a big flat stone to make a raised hearth. In the old days a hole was dug the size of the chimney base. A solid stone wall was then built around the perimeter of the hole and filled with cracked stone. Then a huge flat rock was rolled on top of this base. This was the hearth and chimney base, all in one. My hearth was a lot less work.

Finally, I laid up the stone to form the chimney itself—using the puddled clay liberally—with an adequate opening for the fireplace and for the chimney throat. I am not a stone mason, so I did not try a smoke shelf. For this fireplace I judged it was necessary only to let the smoke out by providing an opening to form a draft. If the shelter had been lower than the surrounding land, a raised chimney cap of stone would have been a good idea, to keep snow and rain off the fire.

As a last touch, I cut off the projecting logs at the shelter's corners. They would have collected water and rotted. The chunks of pine were the start of the shelter's woodpile.

Twenty years ago the materials for one shelter cost about $80. My own labor—some ninety hours—was not valued, because I was using the trial-and-error method. I had not even made a dog house before. My open-front shelters have done their job well. People have camped there during every month of the year. The fact that the shelter has only three sides does not deter winter campers, who hang a blanket over the front. With a nice fire going the shelter is cozy and dry. Occasionally one has visitors: deer mice and porcupines. No bears.

Improving a permanent campsite in woods that are virtually in your own back yard may seem superfluous. Not so, I suggest. Consider the advantages: a pleasant, clean, private camp far from the madding crowd yet readily accessible, convenient, and to be reached without a long, frazzling haul in the family wagon laden with all the gear you haven't forgotten. For children, and for some others, camping is high adventure whatever its venue. You'll have fun, and if you don't, you just walk back home.

VIII | 🌲🌲

Conclusions

I HAVE ENJOYED writing this little book. For thirty years and more I have lived and learned and tried to practice the ideals of modern woodlot forestry and management according to the land use ethic I have attempted to describe here. Putting those ideals down on paper and trying to advise readers how they may be realized has firmed my conviction that man has gotten off on the wrong foot in his approach to his own habitat because he has pretended that he is master of the universe and must dominate all other life forms and bend them to his use.

Our megalomania did no great harm to the planet before the present century. Oh, yes, we could and did burn the woods and foul the waters; and we went in for sod busting, clear cutting, and monoculture, resulting in erosion. But even with these transgressions we hadn't the ability to waste the earth on the scale we can today (and, of course, we hadn't the weaponry that might destroy it utterly at a stroke). Today we burn fossil fuels—our energy capital, really—at a profligate rate, altering the climate and despoiling air and water. We are busily cutting the rain forests without regard to their function in climate making. Everywhere we allow forest land to be sacrificed wastefully for real estate development.

It is not, however, as though we were ignorant of the consequences of our abuse of our own habitat, the earth. We know—or we can easily learn—what will come of our wasteful ways: depleted, eroded cropland; dirty, unhealthy air and water; a dreary landscape in which we can find neither pleasure nor rest. We continue our disastrous course in spite of our knowledge that it is disastrous.

But we don't have to. The beginnings of wisdom are often small, and one of them can be found right here, in our treatment of small woodlots. I can envision a mild, modest antidote to our global madness and waste if woodlot owners take up the idea that each one will spend some time improving his own corner. I find it heartening that, in doing so, we can make a small difference. Small woodlots can play an important part in our survival. They can, as we have seen, ameliorate local climates, moderating winds and floods and providing clean water while combating erosion and siltation. They shelter a variety of plants and animals, increasing biologic strength through diversity and affording resorts of beauty and serenity to all who need them. And they yield wood—the most widely useful material for human purposes that the earth has to give—and other products for our employment and profit.

Right woodlot management, on the principles suggested in this book, can allow individuals working alone or in small groups to make real improvements in an important part of our common environment by helping preserve healthy, productive forests for future generations who will, I hope, be wiser than we are about caring for the whole earth. Right woodlot management, today, means treating forests as complex biological entities rather than as mere timber factories. It means promoting diversity and thrift, making every product of the woodlot find its use. It means working slowly and carefully, working to a plan, working with a trained forester. It means working with the care appropriate to a task that has a small contribution to make toward the goal of a more prosperous world for us all. Finally, it means pausing, taking stock, admiring, and enjoying this, our handiwork.

INDEX

mattock, 86–87
Meylan pruning saw, 60, *illus.* 61, 89, *illus.* 90
money from woodlot:
  and clear cutting, 32
  and exploitation of resources, 27, 31–32, 52
  by using every discard, 19
  see also products of woodlot
monoculture forest:
  and clear cutting, 32
  susceptibility to disease, insects, etc., 17
  and tree planting, 85

native trees, collection of (arboretum), 18, 109–11, *illus.* 111

oak, commercial uses of, 42
orchard, and wildlife island, 119

peavey, *illus.* 62, 63
  and hung-up tree, 76 and *illus.*
  and limbing, 78
peelers (for veneer), 6, 42 and *illus.*, 43
piling stock, 18, 43, *illus.* 44
pine, red, *illus.* 44, *illus.* 94
  as piling stock, 43
  site for, 85
  thinnings, 19
pine, white:
  site for, 85
  thinnings, 19
pioneer tree species, 17, *illus.* 49, 84
planting trees, 84–88, *illus.* 87
  depth, 88
  method, 86–87 and *illus.*
  selection of species, 85–86
  spacing, 87–88
poll axe, *illus.* 57
poplar (popple):
  as fuel wood, 41
  as pioneer, 51
  as pulp or kindling, 45
  value of, 43, 45
porcupines:
  and cuprinol preservative, 95
  tree damage by, 47
precipitation, needed by woodlot, 6, 8
predators, 119
prices for woods, 43
products of woodlot, 26–27
profit (economic) from woodlot:
  and clear cutting, 32
  and exploitation of resources, 27, 31–32, 52
  by using every discard, 19
  see also products of woodlot

pruning, *illus.* 24, 88–92, *illus.* 90
  how much to do, 92
  Tarzan method, 61
  timing of, 91–92
pruning saw, 60, *illus.* 61, 89, *illus.* 90
pulp saw, 60 and *illus.*
pulpwood, 41, 52

raccoons, habitat of, 47
reclamation of open land, by trees, *illus.* 50, 51, 84
  see also pioneer tree species
recreational uses of woodlot, 27, 30–31, 52–53, 109–27 and *illus.*
  aesthetic aspects, 30–31
  arboretum, 18, 109–11, *illus.* 111
  campsites, 121, 123, 125–27
  motorized vehicles, 30
  trails, 120–21
  wildlife habitat, 27, 32, 111–20, *illus.* 114
roads, 96–97, *illus.* 98, 99–101, *illus.* 98–100
  bridges, 104 and *illus.*, 105, 107
  construction of, 101–105, *illus.* 102, *illus.* 104, *illus.* 106
  culverts, 103–104
  ditching, 103
  laying out, 99–101
  leveling, *illus.* 106
  water bars, 101–103, *illus.* 102
  and wet places, 47, 104–105
row thinning, 93

safety measures:
  axe, sharp, 58–59
  for chainsaws, 69, 80
  clothing, protective, *illus.* 66, 67
  for limbing, 77–80
  for tree felling, 70–71
sawlogs, selecting trees for, *illus.* 41, 42
saws, *see* chainsaw; hand saws
seedlings, planting, 86–88, *illus.* 87
sharpening:
  axes, 58–59
  chainsaw, 69
shelter for campsite, 123, *illus.* 124, 125–27
shoot borer (white pine weevil), 87
single-species forest:
  and clear cutting, 32
  susceptibility to disease, insects, etc., 17
  and tree planting, 85
size:
  of land parcels, 14–15
  of woodlot, 5–6